Dedications

For Rosie, Ted and Beatrix – from Jeff
To Margaret, Gillian and Dafydd – from Wyn

Dylan Thomas:
The Pubs

 Mermaids and White Horses

JEFF TOWNS

Original illustrations by Wyn Thomas

First impression: 2013
© Jeff Towns, Wyn Thomas & Y Lolfa Cyf., 2013

Cover photograph: copyright Nora Summers/Dylans Bookstore Collection

Cover & book design: Y Lolfa

ISBN (paperback edition): 978 1 84771 693 4
Hardback edition: 978 1 84771 816 7

Printed on acid-free and partly recycled paper
and published and bound in Wales by
Y Lolfa Cyf., Talybont, Ceredigion SY24 5HE
e-mail ylolfa@ylolfa.com
website www.ylolfa.com
tel 01970 832 304
fax 832 782

Acknowledgements

THIS BOOK, quite fittingly, was conceived in a pub in Wales: In a bar in Cardiff Bay to be precise. It was some four years ago when Dylan Thomas's centenary still seemed way off in the future. I was with my friend Wyn Thomas, the illustrator of this book. It was all his idea. We were drowning our sorrows after getting nowhere with yet another television commissioner. As I recall, Wyn pulled a sheaf of colourful architectural drawings out of his briefcase and spread them on the pub table; I had no idea he was a skilled draughtsman or artist of any kind: his intriguing drawings were all exquisite studies of Swansea pubs. "We should do a book together about Dylan's pubs," he said. And over another round of drinks he outlined his well-thought-out notion. Wyn would provide the illustrations and I would write the text, using the archive of books, ephemera and the knowledge I had built up over the course of forty years pursuing the truth and legends surrounding Dylan Thomas, through my bookselling business of Dylans Bookstore Swansea.

It was a great idea. Wyn and I loved pubs and bars for many of the same reasons we thought Dylan Thomas did; for their warmth and comfort; for unexpected encounters of the first, second and third kind; for the "hwyl", in Welsh; for the "craic" in Irish; for the "jolly good times" in English. And you could get beer and wine, and on special occasions, more exotic drinks. Often you could get quite passable food. We quickly warmed to the idea that researching and producing such a book could be good fun. And indeed it was.

But Wyn did more than just draw the pictures, he gobbled up biographies and anthologies about and by Dylan Thomas as fast as I could get them to him, and they came back quickly, but thickened with bright orange post-it notes, flagging up every mention of a pub or pub fuelled incident – which made my task of writing the text so much easier to approach.

Most of these books are listed in the bibliography but I should like to offer a special thanks to Dylan's main biographers – the late Constantine Fitzgibbon and John Ackerman, and to Paul Ferris and Andrew Lycett. Paul Ferris's monumental edition *Dylan Thomas The Collected Letters* was, in many instances, my starting and finishing point.

I would also thank the Swansea-based scholar and academic James A Davies for his studies of the specific topography surrounding Dylan Thomas and his work and his essential *Reference Companion to Dylan Thomas*. Thanks to Gwen Watkins for all the hours of literary chat we have enjoyed over the last forty years – I have learned so much from her and am honoured that she has contributed a foreword to the book.

And final thanks to my wife and family who care for me and tolerate my obsessions.

Jeff Towns, Swansea, 2013

Thanks for guidance and encouragement in the art work to Phil Lewis and to American cousins Judith Stivers, Eric Griffiths, Jennifer and Eric Benson in finding and photographing the pubs and bars in the USA; also thanks to Handel Jones for his advice.

Wyn Thomas, Swansea, 2013

Contents

Foreword

by Gwen Watkins

I FIRST MET Dylan Thomas in a pub – where else? I had heard a great deal about him (almost all adulatory) from my future husband Vernon Watkins, and this meeting was a disappointment. Dylan had come from Waterloo, where he was seeing Caitlin, Llewelyn and the baby Aeron off to her mother's home in Hampshire. He had unfortunately put all the luggage, food, handbag with money and tickets on the wrong train, which promptly moved out, leaving Caitlin and the children stranded on the platform. There had been a scene, or scenes – Caitlin was never one to waste the violent words she stored in such profusion – money had to be telephoned and waited for, the Hampshire train nearly missed, Caitlin and both children screaming – Dylan was not at his best when he arrived at the meeting-place, the famed Cafe Royal. It lived up to its reputation, faded red velvet, Balkan Sobranies, long amber cigarette holders; he did not. All the faded red velvet, the red plush seats, the marble-topped tables, the shades of Wilde and Beardsley, could not hide his dismay.

The next time I met him was in a quieter scene, also in a pub. He had taken Vernon and me to meet Nina Hamnett in her special seat in The Fitzroy Tavern, well away from the hoi-polloi at the bar, from where she reigned as Queen of the Bohemians, waiting for homage in the form of drinks. She was regally polite to Vernon and me, but graciously maternal to Dylan, whom she loved. He was sweetly affectionate, teasing her by hovering on the edge of naughty jokes and limericks. Vernon bought the drinks, but Dylan was the golden boy. Suddenly there was a flurry at the door, and Betty May flounced in, invading Nina's territory, The Fitzroy, instead of occupying her own, which was The Wheatsheaf. Somehow Dylan managed to amuse the two old friends and enemies, but soon took us away, saying in an undertone that he was afraid Aleister Crowley might turn up.

During the last year of the war Vernon and I saw Dylan in various London pubs, always the centre of a crowd, many of whom were associates in his film work, or BBC people, actors, editors, admirers. It was not easy to talk to him apart from these colleagues. Dr Daniel Jones has described how he found it "impossible to detach him from a new circle of acquaintances, some of whom treated me with less than courtesy… as I awkwardly shuffled about on the periphery of that charmed circle". Vernon never minded being at the back of the circle, as long as he could see and listen to Dylan. I used to watch Caitlin, who did mind, and would begin to flirt with someone in uniform, so outrageously at last that Dylan could no longer remain unaware. This usually led to a scuffle between the tall handsome serviceman whom Caitlin had selected and Dylan. Sometimes it ended with the soldier being drawn into the charmed circle and buying drinks all round, occasionally it ended with Dylan getting thrown out. John Prichard and I were once walking past The Wheatsheaf, when the swing doors flew open and Dylan came rolling out, followed by Caitlin, wringing her hands, and saying, "If only Dylan would just once pick on a little man!" But of course it was she who liked tall men.

After the war, Vernon and I went one Saturday to the Blue Boar in Carmarthen to have lunch with Dylan and Caitlin, who were then living at Blaencwm. It was a Saturday, Carmarthen was crowded with farmers. Dylan had already secured a table in the crush of the bar, but when Caitlin arrived with the five-year-old Llewelyn, whom she had just brought from her mother's home in Hampshire, chaos immediately ensued.

You can read the rest of the story in the text but it ended in us eventually being asked to leave. It was the only time in my life that I have been thrown out of a pub, but I still count it something of an honour to have been thrown out between two poets of stature.

I hardly ever went to pubs after our children were born, but we did one Sunday evening meet Dylan and Caitlin in a small country pub which shall be nameless. It was full of the local horsey set, discussing yesterday's gymkhana in high-pitched neighings. Dylan was almost at once cowed and dispirited, and we left after one drink.

Dylan never felt easy with the upper classes, the Old Etonians and university types, which, may be why he did not frequent The Dover Castle, the BBC bolt-hole, until he was himself a frequent and indeed a famous broadcaster. Caitlin has written that pubs were always a home from home for herself and Dylan; and it is significant that he rarely mentions his home at Cwmdonkin Drive, or indeed the Boathouse with any nostalgia. In his radio script *Return Journey* he does not return to the home of his childhood, but to a Swansea pub, and then to Cwmdonkin Park. In the last days of his life, in New York, it was the pubs of his youth he remembered , where the men sang with their arms round each other. His homes were often short-lived rentals, damp conservatories, camping with friends or relations who soon tired of the invasion; and the last years of his short life were embittered by Caitlin's grievances and furies. The Six Bells, the Swiss, the Marquis, the George, the Stag, and the unknown dank little pub where he took Constantine Fitzgibbon the day before he went to America for the last time – these were all home to him, where he found companionship, enjoyment, appreciation, even solitude when he needed it. Without them he would have been a different person indeed.

G M Watkins, 2012

Introduction:

Dylan Thomas and Drink

I first met Dylan, inevitably, in a pub, since pubs were our natural habitat. From that day onwards, we became dedicated to pubs and each other. Pubs were our primary dedication; each other our secondary. But one fit so snugly into the other that they were perfectly complementary.
– Caitlin Thomas, the opening lines of her book *Double Drink Story* (1998)

Here I am, a little fat pub armchair anarchist full of Welsh Guilt.
– Dylan to Mabley Owen his Swansea friend – Dylan would later call the family dog "Mabley".

DYLAN THOMAS liked a drink, but he loved "the pub". His friend Mervyn Levy, who Dylan described as a "Jewish funny drawer with lots to do and say", was with Dylan in nursery school in the Uplands, Swansea and shared with him their first squalid flat in Redcliffe Street London. Mervyn knew Dylan well and he described Dylan as a "congenial pubber". Then he enlarged upon this, declaring:

Thomas was a pubber of genius, warm, generous, humorous, shedding his wit and delectable bawdiness with all the dazzling conviviality of the bubbles winking and bursting in a glass of lager.

This book is not an attempt to sanitise or bowdlerise Dylan's life. The Victorian physician, and moralising editor, Thomas Bowdler, gave us this word after launching his famous expurgated *The Family Shakespeare* into the parlours of Victorian households. Dylan wrote of him:

The plays under his editorship were made fit for the nursery and convent and, to put it in his own delicate words, were purged of those passages considered indelicate or offensive.

Bowdler lived in Swansea and is buried in Mumbles. There is a more-than-likely apocryphal story/legend/myth, that Dylan was once drinking in Mumbles with Wynford Vaughan Thomas, when they decided to visit Bowdler's grave where Dylan proceeded to relieve himself.

It is impossible to take drink out of Dylan's life, but it is possible to reposition it – to see it as nothing so extraordinary, so shameful, and to attempt to prevent it continuing to be such a barrier between readers and Dylan's real importance as a fine poet, story writer and dramatist. One way of doing this is to recognise how much Dylan loved the pub, over and above the drink.

This day is published, in 10 vols. royal 18mo, price 3l. 3s. boards, **THE FAMILY SHAKSPEARE:** in which nothing is added to the original Text: but those words and expressions are omitted which cannot with propriety be read aloud in a Family. By THOMAS BOWDLER, Esq., F. R. S. and S. A. " My great objects in this undertaking are to remove from the writings of Shakspeare, some defects which diminish their value; and, at the same time, to present to the public an edition of his Plays, which the parent, the guardian, and the instructor of youth, may place without fear in the hands of the pupil; and from which the pupil may derive instruction as well as pleasure; may improve his moral principles, while he refines his taste; and without incurring the danger of being hurt with any indelicacy of expression, may learn in the fate of Macbeth, that even a kingdom is dearly purchased, if virtue be the price of acquisition."—Preface. Printed for Longman, Hurst, Rees, Orme, and Brown, London.

Before going on to make observations about Dylan and drink it may be worth recalling the words of his friend and colleague, BBC producer Aneirin Talfan Davies. In his study of Dylan Thomas as a religious poet *Dylan: Druid of the Broken Body* (1964) he has this to say:

> It is only a misunderstanding of the role and function of the poet's vocation which could lead us to believe that a poet's public (or private) misdemeanours invalidate, in any real way, his poetic statements… But ultimately Thomas, like every other poet, will have to be judged as an artist, and not as a saint.

Dylan Thomas saw the pub as a place of refuge; as a place of conviviality, warmth and shelter; as a theatre in which he could always be counted on to perform, and always be guaranteed an audience! It was also a place where he could enjoy a pint or three with old friends or newfound, like-minded pub habitués. For the first half of his life, the Swansea years, the pub provided the setting and impetus for several fine short stories. It was still a rich source later, in New Quay and Laugharne, when he was creating his eccentric cast of characters for his play for voices *Under Milk Wood*.

For Dylan this love of the pub developed early on, and from my own experience of living here in his home town of Swansea, this is still a very common trait among young teenagers of both sexes, who seem to start pubbing well under the legal age limit. Dylan seems to have developed his liking for beer and, more importantly, the pub, in his teens, but was he just following in his father's footsteps?

D J Thomas was a rather austere figure; the black-gowned head of English at the best old-style Boys' Grammar School in Swansea – but he too liked a drink. Pupils were known to comment on his beery breath on a Friday afternoon after he had enjoyed a lunchtime tipple with his closest staffroom colleague. The first official biography of Dylan Thomas was written by one of Dylan's London pub pals, Constantine Fitzgibbon. It was published in 1966, and early in the book, Fitzgibbon includes a very interesting paragraph on D J Thomas and drink:

> At one point it seems D J Thomas decided Dylan, then a boy or a very young man, was drinking too much. According to what Dylan told his friend Alfred Janes at the time, DJ gave his son a talking-to, and what he said both shocked and surprised the young poet. The well respected and reserved schoolmaster told his son that when young, he too had drunk too much: that this had come close to ruining his life: but that by will-power alone he had conquered his self-destructive life.

Fitzgibbon does suggest that this could be one of Dylan's inventions, however his witness, Fred Janes, is a most reliable source. This story does not appear in any later biographies. Paul Ferris, who wrote the classic *Dylan Thomas – The Biography* (1977, revised 2000) glosses over the subject in a couple of sentences:

> It is said that he (DJ) drank to excess when he was young. He certainly drank enough as a schoolmaster to make people smile.

So it is hard for us to speculate on what influence, DJ exerted on his son's attitude to drink. But Swansea town certainly offered ample opportunities for both father and son. The 1928 *Swansea Directory* lists some sixty 'hotels and beer houses', and ten brewery companies. Swansea was one of the largest towns in Wales, known as the Mineral Centre of the World, and vying with Cardiff to be the capital of a country which was no stranger to drink and its excesses. In 1912, just two years before Dylan was born, *The Welsh Gazette*, an Aberystwyth newspaper, published a fierce, red-covered, substantial booklet by T J Rhys entitled *Wales and its Drink Problem*. It documents the total figures for convictions for drunkenness for the period 1905-1910. Cardiff has 735 cases while Swansea racks up a massive 4,715 convictions – a staggering sixfold difference!

Dylan grew up in a society and culture that displayed extreme and dichotomous reactions to alcohol. Throughout Wales, many villages and industrial frontier towns, built around iron and copperworks, quarries, mines, and coalfields, boasted as many pubs as chapels. The anti-drink brigade, made up of Rechabites, Junior Temperance Leagues and The Order of Band of Hope, all had to contend with the boozy culture that prevailed in the country's rugby clubs, miners' institutes and workingmen's clubs. These places, mainly all-male bastions, tolerated and sometimes encouraged and often celebrated heavy binge drinking.

The fact that young Thomas enjoyed the pleasures of the taproom could almost be considered a norm. He first expresses this delight in an early letter to his

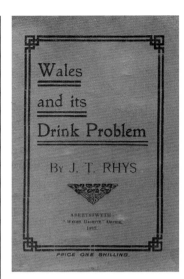

first serious girlfriend, the poet and novelist Pamela Hansford Johnson (who would later marry the novelist C P Snow). Their relationship began by post, with them commenting on each other's poems as they appeared in the Poet's Corner of the London weekly newspaper the *Sunday Referee*. Their letters quickly grew longer and more personal; in a letter dated January 1934, Dylan offers this description of one of his typical Swansea days:

> I read until about twelve or thereabouts… then down the hill to the Uplands (a lowland collection of crossroads and shops) for one (or perhaps two) pints of beer in The Uplands Hotel… then back home for lunch… read all afternoon… continue on a poem or a story… After tea I read or write again… then I go to Mumbles… First I call at The Marine, then The Antelope and then The Mermaid… Thus drifts an average day… Too much thinkin', too much talkin', too much alcohol.

In his later story 'Old Garbo', which was published in his collection of autobiographical short stories *Portrait of the Artist as a Young Dog* (1940), Dylan would offer a lyrical and majestic prose hymn to the rich pleasures of ale which would make any advertising copywriter green with envy:

> I liked the taste of beer, its live white lather, its brass-bright depths, the sudden world through the wet brown walls of the glass, the tilted rush to the lips and the slow swallowing down to the lapping belly, the salt on the tongue, the foam at the corners.

Throughout his life, Dylan's chosen occupations

A certificate the like of which young Thomas never earned!

were not designed to keep him away from drink, far from it; although jobs did seem to choose him rather than being responses to any vocation on his part; his only avowed vocation was to be a poet.

His short-lived employments in Swansea, and later in London and America, were always in jobs in which drink, both during and after work, was a part of the daily routine. Dylan Thomas's school career was a largely unspectacular affair. He only excelled in his studies of English, in debating, in acting in school plays, – contributing to, and eventually editing, the school magazine – and, much more of a surprise, at long-distance running. He won the school athletics mile race twice. In 1931, when Dylan had not yet turned seventeen, his father became resigned to the fact that his son was not interested in, nor would he benefit from, any further education. DJ used his influence and got Dylan a job as a cub reporter on the local paper.

We can learn just how boozy a period this became for the young poet from his story "Old Garbo", which recreates this world in all its sordid detail. In it Dylan recounts his first rite-of-passage night out "on the pop" with an older, well-pickled journo. Although it starts with his prose ode to the joys of beer, the final tone is much more negative in its description of the squalor and drink-related misery he encounters, not least his own violent hangover. But a few years later he writes of his love of this town and its pubs in his radio script *Reminiscences of Childhood* (1943):

> Never was there such a town as ours... for the smell of fish and chips on Saturday nights... for the crowds in

the streets… for the singing that gushed from the smoky doorways of the pubs in the quarters we never should have visited… The reality is there. The fine, live people, the spirit of Wales itself.

His career as a journalist lasted barely a couple of years, but in that time Dylan grew accustomed to spending time in pubs and, when he moved to London in his early twenties, this pattern continued. In London his first career move took him from print into radio broadcasting. Dylan made his first radio broadcast in 1937 when he read poetry for the BBC. He soon began to work regularly for the Corporation in London and he quickly became friends with producers and programme makers such as Louis MacNiece, Roy Campbell and John Arlott, all keen topers. The notion that work could be conducted in the pub once again took hold.

In 1941, another career change saw Dylan move from radio into film. The head of Strand Films, Donald Taylor, employed him as a scriptwriter for both wartime propaganda films and entertainment feature films. Dylan entered yet another milieu where drink and drinking were an accepted part of the working environment. Donald Taylor was later to collaborate with Dylan on the gothic film script based on the nineteenth-century Burke and Hare body snatching case, *The Doctor and the Devils* (1953).

Taylor endorsed this relaxed regime and encouraged an unstructured approach to work. Dylan found himself having to explain this to his new workmate, the eccentric writer Julian Maclaren-Ross. When, after a few days into the job, Maclaren-Ross

Dylan enjoying a game of shove halfpenny in a London pub

was bemused by the erratic comings and goings of a new face around the office (it was Dylan's pal, the Australian novelist Philip Lindsay), he asked Dylan for an explanation and his reply captures the workplace ethos:

> Phil's on the Crippen script… Works at home nowadays and only shows up Fridays to collect his dough.

Taylor, as managing director, would defend his creative staff when the accountants and clerks protested and demanded formal hours and clocking-in; all that mattered to Taylor was that his writers produced good scripts on or near his deadlines. Enjoyable though this was, both Dylan and Maclaren-Ross could have benefited from a more disciplined work ethos. In his much respected chronicle *Memoirs of Forties* (1965), Maclaren-Ross describes his first day at work with Dylan. When the initial formalities, introductions, and general sizing up of each other were over, Dylan suggested they should get down to work on their project; a documentary on the Home Guard. Maclaren-Ross had other ideas:

> We could discuss it over drinks. They'll be open time we get there.

Thus commenced a pub crawl that began in the back bar of the Café Royal on Piccadilly and lasted into the night; Maclaren-Ross writes " we worked our way up Soho in search of Scotch, towards The Wheatsheaf, where we were certain of Scotch ale at any rate". The evening ended with them both well oiled in the Highlander where "they discovered gin". The next morning Dylan was very much under the weather, and it is worth noting that when Ross suggests they keep a bottle of whiskey in the office for just such occasions, Dylan is adamant:

> "Whiskey? *In the office?*" (Dylan) seemed absolutely appalled.
> "Don't be silly. Why not?" But Dylan firmly shook his head. "Not for me. You please yourself of course, but I won't if you don't mind."

Julian Maclaren-Ross was to become one of the great, decadent, lost writers of the 40s, and, like Dylan, his writing career was cut short; he succumbed to the rigours of his lifestyle, dying in 1964, at the age of 52. He rivalled Dylan with his love of bars and pubs, and both were so keen on being the centre of the bar-room's attention that they took to patronising separate pubs, or at least separate bars in the same pub. Although he refused to keep alcohol in the office, it was during this time that Dylan consolidated his reputation as a good and lively drinking companion. He became a well-known fixture around the bars and drinking clubs that he would come to love – the French House, The Helvetia, the Fitzroy and the Wheatsheaf; the Gargoyle and the Mandrake. And by now he had a regular companion; a wife, Caitlin Macnamara (herself no mean imbiber). She later recalls this period in her book *Caitlin, a Warring Absence* (1986):

> His pubbing became relentless. He would go out in the evening with a chrysanthemum in his lapel, pretending to be a queen. He would dress up in fancy clothes saying he was "an actor from the BBC", then offer to bite the caps of bottles of beer if he could have the beer. Some of his pub games were incredibly childish, if not embarrassing. One called cats and dogs: he would get down on his hands and knees and crawl round a bar, biting people's ankles… He would pour drinks into other people's pockets: and once I heard he unbuttoned his trousers and offered a girl his penis… [he] also had an enormous repertoire of obscene songs, dirty limericks and 'blue' stories… Dylan had acquired a reputation as the pub fool and he had to keep it at all costs.

On a very recent visit to Laugharne a local no-good-boyo surreptitiously palmed a scrap of paper into my pocket with a nod and wink, like it was a wrap of some secret local narcotic. When I got to look at it, it turned out to be a photocopy of an original scatological verse by Dylan Thomas entitled "Plaint

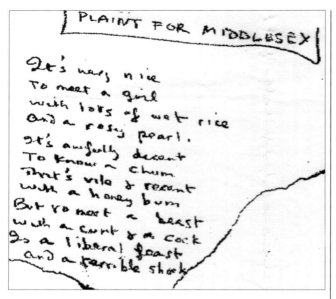

'golden singers and the sulphurous hermaphrodites'.

And in one of his introductions to an American reading in 1953 (recorded on one of his Caedmon LP's) he postulates an example of the kind of "more interesting question" he would like to be asked:

> If every hermaphrodite were a schizophrene which half would you take?

The recording indicates that the audience's response was of loud laughter which was also what greeted another scatological quip he threw into another introduction at the Poetry Centre while introducing William Plomer's poem *The Flying Bum*:

> I should explain that "bum" to an Englishman does not mean what it means to an American. "Bum" means "fanny", and "fanny" does not mean to an American what it means to an Englishman though geographically it's quite close.

Dylan's next, and final, gainful occupation, was as a peripatetic lecturer on, and performer of, poetry. He had gained a reputation from his work at the BBC as a gifted and well-respected reader, both of his own work and that of other poets. He had also been involved in some large public readings, one of which, in May 1946, was at London's Wigmore Hall. Dylan joined a stellar group of leading poets which included T S Eliot, Edith Sitwell and Walter de la Mare. The audience consisted of the great and the good and the royal family; the Queen, Princess Elizabeth (later Queen Elizabeth II) and Princess Margaret were in

for Middlesex". I had never seen it before but is an example of one of Dylan's smutty pub poems that Caitlin speaks of. Dylan seems to have something of a fixation with hermaphrodites. His early poem, "Then was my Neophyte", a poem he considered the best in his second collection, *Twenty-Five Poems* (1936), has the lines

> *My sea hermaphrodite*
> *Snail of man in His ship of fires*
> *That burn the bitten decks.*

In his prose piece "Prologue to Adventure", which was first published in the first issue of Wales magazine in 1937, Dylan writes of:

attendance. Dylan read Blake's "Tyger Tyger", D H Lawrence's "Snake" and his own "Fern Hill". The *Times* carried a review of the event in which Thomas's performance was praised over that of Eliot and Sitwell.

By the late 1940s what Dylan was really looking for was some kind of lucrative reading tour or lectureship in America. In 1945 he wrote to the American editor and anthologist Oscar Williams of his desire for:

> a little ladleful from the gravy pots over there – a lick of the ladle, the immersion of a single hair in the rich shitbrown cauldron… I want to come over to America. How could I earn a living? I can read aloud, through sonorous asthma, with pomp… I can lecture… I can write scripts.

Dylan's letter detailing his choice of poems to read to the Queen – current and future

Eventually, through the dedication of John Malcolm Brinnin, the American poet infatuated with Dylan and his poetry, such a lecture tour became a reality. In his remarkable memoir *Dylan Thomas in America* (1956), Brinnin recalls:

> Without his knowledge I had made a number of attempts to have him invited to America… But all these efforts were unsuccessful. When, in 1949, I was offered the directorship of The Poetry Center of the YM-YWHA in New York, I accepted this position with one thought in my mind: at last I could myself invite Dylan Thomas to come to America. My first act in my new position was to write to him. His reply was an immediate warm acceptance, not only of my invitation but of my offer to do whatever I could to make his American visit a success.

Dylan left for his first visit on February 21st, 1950 and, with Brinnin's help, he eventually undertook three extensive lecture tours across the length and breadth of North America. The first was three months long, the second in 1952, when Caitlin accompanied him, was of two-and-half-months and the third, in 1953, lasted a little more than a month. His fourth short and tragic final tour, later the same year, lasted little more than two weeks before he died in St Vincent's Hospital in New York City on November 9th, 1953.

On these epic tours Dylan gave more than a hundred public performances as he criss-crossed the continent from New York to Los Angeles and from Florida to Montreal. And after almost every reading there was the obligatory faculty party or elaborate dinner where Dylan, already exhausted, was expected to perform yet again, this time while being urged to consume constant alcohol. Now the drinks came in the guise of large and elaborate American cocktails. The measures in which spirits were served in American bars (and homes) were much larger than anything Dylan had encountered in the UK, and this fact alone played no small part in his downfall.

The BBC Wales online arts website has a substantial Dylan Thomas section. The biography section has one page, just headed 'Dylan Thomas: Alcohol', and it begins with the stark statement:

The Dylan Thomas legend is soaked to the skin in drink.

There can be no doubt that by the time Dylan Thomas reached America this statement was true of the legend, but by then, with tragic consequences, it was also true of his life. By the 1950s the "Dylan Thomas Legend" was well established. It consisted of a heady mixture of fact and fabrication, much of it promulgated by Dylan himself. It positioned him firmly in the popular imagination as the archetypal romantic, bohemian, creative artist and tortured poet. Features in picture magazines and the popular press had seen lazy journalists prefix every mention of Dylan Thomas with the clichéd "hard-drinking poet" or "boozy poet". Furthermore this reputation seemed to have crossed the Pond and had become prevalent in America, but like a proverbial Chinese whisper it seemed to have been embellished and exaggerated as it travelled across the ocean with him. This contemporary letter to Vernon Watkins from respected American playwright, Bob Hivor, offers telling examples of this phenomenon.

In his biography of Dylan Thomas, Paul Ferris sums it up succinctly:

But death at thirty-nine, more or less in the arms of a mistress, and awash with alcohol, freeze-framed him in people's imagination as a poet who lived and died like one: lyrical, dissolute and struck down in his prime. His story is more complex. Even the climactic scenes have been tinkered with. The final 'eighteen straight whiskies' are a myth. The mistress, though real enough, is evidence of casual infidelity, not of a great womaniser; he was too disorganised for that. Nor was he in his prime. By that October day in 1953, he was spiritually as well as physically wasted.

```
Dear Vernon,
          "Do you know any Dylan Thomas stories?" seems to have become
a common question where the benighted literary people around here--and I
suppose all over America--gather.  It seems there are many and since they
skip split up into new stories like a cell dividing soon there will probably
be many more.  A few:
          At a party in his honor at Harvard (or Princeton? or Williams? or
Connecticut Womens?) Peter Vierick, an interesting poet and a Professor of
History, brought several of his books as gifts to Thomas.
          "Here is my book Terror and Decorum."
          Thomas, "Ahh."  Complete indifference.
          "Here is my book so and so."
          "Ohh." More indifference.
          "And here is my latest book Conservatism Revisited."
          Thomas: "Better it should never have been visited at all."

          He was asked by an old lady about political prospects in England
and he replies, "All I'm interested in is breasts!"

          To a comely coed at Radcliffe (or Vassar, or Smith) he says,
"Oh to be suckled at those breasts!"

          At one point he claims to be the only male British poet.

          Professor so and so says to him at a Railroad station. "I am
professor so and so of the welcoming committee come here to welcome
you."  Thomas, goggle eyed and belching on strange beers, "I'm
glad you're Professor so and so...I'm glad there's a welcoming
committee...I'm glad your're here...I'm glad."
```

Thomas's shockers "all I'm interested in is breasts", "Oh to be suckled at those breasts", "I am the only male British poet"

"He sped into the drinking dark"
– from Dylan's poem *Ballad of the Long-Legged Bait*

THE SORDID DETAILS of the events that led to Dylan's untimely and unseemly death in New York City have already been chronicled and dissected, second-guessed and analysed in too many books. Fitzgibbon's gives us just a page or two and little detail. The biographies of Ferris and Lycett tell us perhaps all we need to know. George Tremlett's book with Caitlin, and his biography of Dylan, were then followed by his book *The Death of Dylan Thomas* (1997), written with an American physician James Nashold, containing a detailed analysis of Dylan's final week in New York. In 1998 the late great poet, Adrian Mitchell, provided some respite and sanity in his beat-poetry rap *Who Killed Dylan Thomas?* (complete with remarkable, but typically gruesome illustrations, by Ralph Steadman).

Then a new name enters the fray, David N Thomas, whose numerous meticulously researched articles, culminated in his obsessively detailed book *Fatal Neglect: Who Killed Dylan Thomas?* (2008).

The sum total of all these words suggest that, although Dylan's excessive consumption of alcohol was significant, there were other crucial contributing factors to the tragedy that unfolded; Dylan's overall physical and mental health at the time; the administration of various drugs by his New York doctor, Milton Feltenstein. Dylan had already gained a taste for what he called Feltenstein's "winking needle" but on that last night it was the steroid ACTH by injection and, on his third visit, the half a grain of morphine sulphate which appear to have sent Dylan into a fatal coma.

The "eighteen straight whiskies" has been pretty much discounted as another of Dylan's hyperbolic boasts; his friend Ruthven Todd went out the day after his collapse and checked in all the local bars, no-one seemed to recall a prolonged visit from Dylan, let alone such prolific consumption of whiskey. I think it is worth noting that towards the end of *Under Milk Wood*, which Dylan was working on at this time, the character, Cherry Owen, boasts of having, "downed seventeen pints of flat, warm, thin, Welsh, bitter beer" – seventeen beers… close to eighteen whiskies?

All attempts to suggest "missing hours in the narrative", medical incompetence, cover-ups and the plethora of lurid rumour and bizarre conspiracy theories surrounding Dylan's death are of no interest. They are prurient at best, and evil and disrespectful at their worst. It is worth quoting here a recent extreme, but by no means unique, example of the Chinese-whisper effect that blights Dylan Thomas. This from the Irish folk singer, (so we can expect an overdose of blarney). Liam Clancy's *Memoirs of an Irish Troubadour* (2002):

> For us the White Horse Tavern was the poetic singing centre of the village. In 1953 Dylan Thomas had taken his last drink there, or rather his last thirty-six drinks. Legend has it that the Welsh poet, overwhelmed by fame, took refuge in the long-shoreman's bar on Hudson Street. The

doctors told him that even one more whiskey would do in his liver, so he set up a pyramid of thirty-six shot glasses of whiskey on the counter of the White Horse bar. He looked a long time at the pyramid, contemplating. Then he took the top shot glass off the pile, downed it, and with suicidal certainty drank glass after glass until the pyramid was demolished. He was rushed to St Vincent's Hospital a few blocks away but never recovered consciousness. In the end he *did* go gentle into that good night.

Utter piffle, in my opinion. I believe that Vernon Watkins said the only right words about Dylan's death:

> The true tragedy of Dylan's death is that he died.

Dylan Thomas lived for just under four decades and it seems to me that throughout these years his use of alcohol got steadily more dangerous and ultimately fatal. This may be simplistic, but he certainly did not drink in his first decade. In his second, spent largely in Swansea, he began to get a taste for beer, but also began his lifelong love affair with the pub. By December of 1934 Dylan is writing to Glyn Jones, describing his current "lean period", leading to "scanty meals in cafes", which, he explains:

> are scanty not for the reason of utter penury... but for the sake of the demon alcohol who has become too close and heavy a friend for some time now.

The third decade, spent largely in London, saw the pressures of the war, and the growing influence of his new friends in the BBC and film world, combine to increase his intake of beer. In his book *War Like a Wasp: The Lost the Decade of the Forties* (1989), Andrew Sinclair (who directed the film of *Under Milk Wood* and wrote a good biography of Dylan, *Dylan Thomas: Poet of His People* 1975) emphasises the importance of the pub:

> The forced gregariousness, the necessary intimacy of writers and artists in those war years discovered its milieu in the pubs, which also had their golden age.

Theodora Fitzgibbon, who was married to Constantine Fitzgibbon and was a respected cookery writer, wrote a very perceptive memoir *With Love; an Autobiography 1938-1946* (1982). Dylan and Caitlin spent many evenings with "Con and Theo" in the London pubs they loved. Theodora's memoir does much to capture the London of the 40s, and she says this about pub life:

> They were the only places in wartime London where one could entertain and be entertained cheaply, and find the companionship badly needed during the war. For people of our age with no solid, regular accounts behind us, it was difficult to come by even a bottle of sherry... Many middle-aged couples used to drinking at home found their only source of supply was the pubs. Bombs dropping on London could not be heard when one was in them and the company lessened apprehension. I loved pubs, they were new to me and I liked being able to find friends I wanted to see in certain places at certain times. Dylan had previously pointed out to me that the link between host and guest was a tenuous one, but that it never arose if one met in a pub.

The fourth and last decade of Dylan's life saw his financial and domestic situation getting steadily worse and his solution, a series of extensive lecture tours to America, in fact precipitated the beginnings of his end. His marriage and relationship with Caitlin were irreparably damaged by his affair with the American writer Pearl Kazin during his first tour in 1950, and this tour also saw the beginnings of his consumption of whiskey. Old Grand-Dad Bourbon became his drink of choice and he was gifted bottles of the stuff by his dubious new American friends and acquaintances.

It is true that the increase in Dylan's drinking coincides with a decline in his ability to write poetry. Yet this is not a straightforward equation. In his second decade, between the age of sixteen and twenty, Dylan produced more than half the poems that make up his *Collected Poems 1934-1952*. These poems were mostly written in the notebooks that Dylan sold to a London bookseller when he was twenty-six, the age at which his great literary hero John Keats died. Perhaps he was aware that this incredible surge of testosterone-fuelled productivity was never to be repeated.

However, although the number of poems reduced dramatically, those poems that he did complete in the second half of his life include some of his finest and most famous – the war poem *A Refusal to Mourn the Death, by Fire, of a Child in London*, *The Hunchback in the Park*, *Fern Hill*, *Do Not Go Gentle Into That Good Night*, *Over Sir John's Hill*, *Poem in October* and *In Country Heaven*. This decline in quantity may be partially attributed to his drinking but he also found himself having to write and perform to try and make enough money to keep his growing family at the same time as he was giving talks and lectures, appearing on the radio and also producing his ground-breaking

Dylan's favourite American whiskey

radio scripts and plays and writing short stories. There was not much time left for poetry.

The critic James A Davies, suggests that on this first visit to New York, Dylan:

> the habitual beer drinker, drank more spirits in his first three days in the city than, probably, in his life up to that point.

On his second trip, with Caitlin, Dylan Thomas revisited Chicago to give a reading. His hostess for the visit was a local grandee, Ellen Borden Stevenson, the former wife of the politician Adlai Stevenson. It was also she who would generously offer to pay for the best independent specialists to treat Dylan as he lay dying in St Vincent's Hospital a little more than a year later. Ellen had arranged for one of Dylan's favourite American authors, Nelson Algren, to join them. Algren's controversial novel about drug addiction *The Man with the Golden Arm* had won the first National Book Award in 1950. The meeting went well enough, but Algren was moved to comment on the drinking of both Caitlin, who he thought had a real problem and was to be pitied, and Dylan of whom he remarked:

I was neither poet nor lush enough to appreciate him fully. You have to feel a certain desperation about everything either to write like that or to drink like that.

In a later review of John Malcolm Brinnin's *Dylan Thomas in America,* which Algren wrote for the *Chicago Sun Times* in 1956, he writes:

This reviewer's goods being prose, I was not intimately acquainted with the product being handled by the poetry trade in the fall of 1951. I felt myself on more solid ground in discussing beer than the avant-garde. My first concern, therefore, in meeting Dylan and Caitlin Thomas was to limit the conversation to the virtues of local brands of malt and hops. Discoursing quietly yet commandingly... I advised my guests of my work with Michelob, Budweiser, Edelweiss and Schlitz. I would have done better to stick to poetry. Thomas's own studies had been extended to Persian, Icelandic, Manx, Mexican, Frisian, Turkish and Moorish beers. He was a philosopher of beer, a prophet of beer, a John Foster Dulles of beer. Outclassed, I made one last weak try.

"Anyhow," I told him, "I once knew a man named Champagne who drunk nothing but beer."

"I knew a man named Beers who drank nothing but champagne," Thomas assured me, I decided I liked him whatever his trade, and we went off in search of either beer or champagne. We found both.

Dylan Thomas – "Philosopher of Beer": how he would have enjoyed that sobriquet. Algren also offers a more serious and poignant judgement:

Before he died it was at last borne in upon me that I had been greatly privileged. I had been with a great man, the only great man I had ever known.

One of Dylan's closest American friends was the poet Theodore Roethke, who shared with Dylan a love of bars and drink. He summed up his Welsh friend thus:

He had been built up to me as a great swill-down drinker, a prodigious roaring boy out of the Welsh caves. But I never knew such a one. Some bubbly or Guinness or just plain beer, maybe; and not much else.

Bernard Mitchell's charming image of Dan in his local, The Newton, 1966

On his final trip to America in late October of 1953, Dylan's last public appearance was on a panel assembled by the prestigious Cinema 16 group to discuss "Poetry and Film". One of his co-panellists was the great American playwright, Arthur Miller, famously once married to another great twentieth-century live-fast-die-young icon, Marilyn Monroe. In his autobiography *Timebends: A life* (1987), Miller writes about sitting in a room in the Chelsea Hotel, and as memories flood back he offers just one short, poignant paragraph about Dylan Thomas:

> It was not only Marilyn on my mind; in this very hotel early in the fifties, I had sat in one of these tall grey rooms trying to fathom Dylan Thomas as he methodically made his way out of this world, a young man who with a week's abstinence would have been as healthy as a pig. Much later, when I read his confessional about his father, it seemed to me that he was throttling himself for having conquered fame with his art while the sweet father, a writer-teacher, remained an unknown failed man. Thomas was making amends by murdering the gilt he had stolen from the man he loved.

It is worth tempering these observations from London and American sources by looking at what his Swansea friends have written and said about Dylan Thomas and drink. Dan Jones – whose initial schoolboy meeting with Dylan is described in Dylan's short story, "The Fight", published in *Portrait of the Artist* – was a close lifelong friend and no stranger to the pub himself. Dan lived for the latter part of his life just along the road from my house in Newton, above Mumbles here in Swansea. I could set my watch by Danny's daily shuffles from his house to The Newton pub for a gentle liquid lunch, then back home, before repeating the same journey in the late afternoon.

A painting of Dan still hangs in the bar of the pub. Dan was a polymath; he may well have been a genius; he was a literary and musical prodigy and as schoolboys he and Dylan collaborated in writing poetry and prose. His prodigious linguistic skills – he knew many languages including Chinese and Russian

– saw him conscripted to Bletchley Park for code-breaking duties during the war years.

Dan's book *My Friend Dylan Thomas* (1977) is an intriguing account of their friendship and contains Dan's reflections on Dylan and drink. It begins:

Much has been written about Dylan and his drinking; most of it is misleading.

He then explains:

To the teetotaller, no doubt Dylan would seem a heavy drinker… Most of my friends drank every day a fair amount of alcohol… By their standards, Dylan was a steady habitual, not heavy hardened drinker.

He goes on to discuss what he means by "heavy" and "hardened" and concludes:

Unlike hardened cases, he was exclusively a social drinker.

He also declares that he liked drinkers:

because you encountered their true characters which, far from being inscrutable, were often more clearly revealed by alcohol.

Dylan's other close Swansea friend was fellow poet Vernon Watkins who, although not a teetotaller, was not a drinking man. For him a dip in the icy sea in Hunt's Bay just below his Gower home was a far more enticing prospect than a visit to a smoky bar.

Vernon wrote a great deal on Dylan's poetry and

Vernon Watkins: happy in Hunt's Bay, Gower

prose but very rarely ventured into discussions of his life and character. He had a deep and abiding love and respect for Dylan and his work. The two poets corresponded throughout their lives and in 1957 Vernon edited Dylan's letters for publication in *Dylan Thomas Letters to Vernon Watkins*. His wonderful sensitive and informing commentary on the letters indicates the depth of their friendship and Vernon's complete dedication to Dylan – both the man and his work. If you look at the title page of the book it has two publishers – J M Dent and Faber and Faber.

This is very unusual, but there is a reason. Dent were, and still are, Dylan's publishers but they also published John Malcolm Brinnin's *Dylan Thomas in America* and Vernon despised the book. For Vernon, Brinnin's account of his dear friend's last few years was too harsh and brutal. It was too much for him to take; he was in denial about much of what he read and heard. For Vernon, Dylan was social drinker who occasionally had a few too many; he was never the drunken bore that Brinnin describes. He was so appalled by Brinnin's book that when Dent approached him to publish Dylan's letters Vernon flatly refused – he would have nothing to do with the insensitive morons who could publish what he saw as such an evil, unbalanced book. Only after long and protracted negotiations and diplomacy did he acquiesce, and then only if his publishers, Faber and Faber, handled his input and appeared on the title page – his devotion to Dylan made any engagement with Dent untenable.

In an unpublished draft for a review article on Brinnin's book written for Stephen Spender's *Encounter*, Vernon writes:

> To imagine Dylan Thomas as a teetotaller is a sad picture, and this he would not have become, but he was not an alcoholic either. Beer was to him a necessary social medium. Spirits were not, and it is my belief that this unnecessary social adjunct, which is the medium of American hospitality, hastened his death.

And his wife Gwen Watkins adds:

> Dylan did not always need drink – or at least not alcohol. When he was at ease, relaxed, and drinking only beer, nothing went wrong, but if he was under pressure or anxious and began to drink spirits, then trouble began.

All the members of the group of writers, artists and musicians who used to meet occasionally in Swansea's Kardomah Café were interesting characters but some stood out. I was lucky enough to meet and become friends with a good few of them. One in particular was Charles Fisher. He was in school with Dylan, where he was briefly Dylan's first "wife"! In the all-boys school, the drama group had to resort to a certain amount of cross-dressing in their productions.

When they performed Galsworthy's *Strife*, Dylan played the lead character, the strike-breaker Roberts, and Charlie Fisher played his wife. After school Charlie joined Dylan as a journalist on the local paper the *South Wales Daily Post*, now the *South Wales Evening Post*, where he wrote news, arts and a fishing column. Although the phrase is overused, Charles was a real character: he once arrived at the newspaper offices on horseback, kitted out in jodhpurs and spurs and nonchalantly proceeded to tether his steed to a lamp-post on Swansea's busy thoroughfare. He would later travel to Spain where he was adopted by the real Gypsies in Andalusia, who adored him and taught him to play Flamenco guitar (I know this because he serenaded me in fine style when I visited!).

When I met him he was approaching ninety, but he was still a fit and handsome man who drove a bright red vintage Jaguar at great speed down the dusty roads of rural Ontario where he had ended up after a career as Canada's "Hansard"; he was employed as the stenographer who took down the proceedings of Canada's Parliament in Ottawa for many decades.

Charlie loved life and still lived it to the full at ninety but he was not a big drinker. In an interview with Colin Edwards he said of Dylan:

> … he could drink far more than I could at the time and far more consistently… he was mainly a drinker of mild beer.

It was the discovery that there were such things as treble whiskies, which he told me about in an awed voice one day… he asked me once when we were probably just out of school, "Do you like beer" and I said, no, I don't. But he said "Well I *like* it, that's the trouble I like it." He really liked the stuff… I never saw him drunk. It is extraordinary, that I remember knowing him for a long time… before he drank anything at all except tea or ginger ale. He must have started drinking on the *Evening Post*… in the evening, I didn't see him… We went dancing but not Dylan, Dylan was around the pubs in Swansea and there he got the tales for many stories.

And finally Bert Trick, young Dylan's political guru, has this to say:

Many were the times I skipped out of 5 Cwmdonkin Drive, my arms full of books, my head full of stars and feet of feathers. I didn't walk down the hill to my home, I was levitated. There was no need for strong drink, we were intoxicated with words – ideas and words.

And what do we learn from Dylan's work about drink? He wrote in detail about local pubs and characters in his short stories. The pubs sound none too appealing, and the excesses of drinking that goes on is neither praised nor celebrated. Only in one of his stories, the late and much loved tale, "The Outing", which was originally known just as "A Story", does he offer a glorious celebration of male drinking camaraderie. "A Story" was written for the BBC; Dylan read it live, on camera, on August 10th, 1953. It was one of only two TV programmes he recorded. Sadly neither exists today.

Charles Fisher

This story is an account, through the eyes of a young boy, of a typical Welsh, all-male, all-day pub-crawl through West Wales, by charabanc. It is also one of his greatest comic works, full of wit, humour and verbal slapstick, and tells of a bus full of men getting roaring drunk and ending up spreadeagled, en masse, in a field. What intrigues me is that although many commentators criticise Dylan for his love of beer and pubs – this story celebrates exactly that behaviour

THE OUTING
Dylan Thomas
Illustrated by Paul Cox

The cover of the children's illustrated edition of "The Outing"
While Dylan is castigated by his detractors for this kind of
behaviour – we are happy to present it to our children

and became a well-received BBC television feature and, perhaps even more surprisingly, was published as a book for children with charming, but explicit illustrations, by a very well-respected illustrator, Paul Cox.

This seems to illustrate just how ambivalent we are, as a society, about drink and its effects. *Under Milk Wood* is generally joyous and mischievous about pubs and drinking. Mr Waldo's drunken behaviour is severely criticised by the gossiping, clecking housewives:

> Every Saturday… He hasn't got a leg… And carrying on… What he'll do for drink… falling in the gutter, talking to the lamp-post… Using language… singing in the w.

Cherry Owen's weekly inebriated return from the pub is related by his wife with resigned good humour:

> Remember last night? In you reeled my boy, as drunk as a deacon with a big wet bucket and a fish-frail full of stout and you l ent, sprawling and bawling and the floor was all flagons and eels.

Llareggub's local pub, The Sailors Arms, is celebrated for its clock:

> The ship's clock in the bar says half-past eleven. Half-past eleven is opening time. The hands of the clock have stayed still at half-past eleven for fifty years. It is always opening time in The Sailors Arms.

When Cherry Owen goes in the pub, and Sinbad the barman asks "what'll you have?", Cherry replies, "Too much."

In his poetry Dylan Thomas rarely writes about drink and drinking but offers us two, wonderfully inventive similes to illustrate the effect of drink, which suggest, at least some first-hand experience:

Drunk as a vineyard snail – from *How Shall My Animal*
Drunk as a new dropped calf – from *Lament*

And Dylan left us his own witty aphorism on drink:

An alcoholic is someone you don't like who drinks as much
as you do.

In a letter to Vernon Watkins describing a
recent trip to Ireland Dylan celebrates his discovery
of Guinness but also offers an indication of his
knowledge of Welsh history and folklore:

we drank Seithenyns of porter and Guinness.

Seithenyn, in Welsh folklore, was the Welsh prince
whose love of drink caused a village to be drowned.
    When Dylan left school and became a journalist on
local papers, one of his most interesting achievements
was a series of six articles for the *Herald of Wales*, "The
Poets of Swansea". He quickly nails his colours to the
mast when he praises George Borrow for the fact that
"He praises the ale" of Swansea in *Wild Wales*. When
he writes about a minor local poet, Mr S C Gamwell,
Dylan chooses to highlight his particular poem
about Ellen Sweeney, "one time Queen of Swansea
night-life". The poem celebrates her "two hundred
and twenty fifth conviction for drunkenness"! Dylan
quotes a stanza of Gamwell's ode; the last line could be
Dylan's own epitaph:

Convicted Sir? I've been convicted
Two hundred and twenty-five times.

The Welsh artist Brian Rees made this wonderful new dust
jacket design featuring Dylan in the Sailor's Arms

Lord love you, you need not shrink from me –
It wasn't for very dark crimes.
I never did nothing to no one
To hurt 'em. Some high people wink
At sins in themselves just as dreadful
My fault is a drop too much to drink.

But his article on Llewellyn Prichard, an eccentric
writer of what is considered the first Welsh novel
Twm Shon Cati (1828), is the most revealing. Dylan is
obviously smitten by Prichard and describes him thus:

… he would have been a remarkable figure… being six foot tall and proportionately broad, with thin features and lustrous eyes. He had lost his nose in a duel many years before… and now, comically sticking from his tragedian's face was a large upturned wax nose. "Would to God," he once said, pointing at his nose, "the second artist had been as clever as the first".

Prichard would die in drunken poverty in a Swansea slum surrounded by his books and manuscripts when his candle set his clothes and him on fire. Dylan ends his article:

He failed to be great, but he failed with genius.

Once again this could be Dylan's epitaph, but it is his opening paragraph which offers us a startling and remarkable example of Dylan's uncanny prescience:

No one can deny that the most attractive figures in literature are always those around whom a world of lies and legends has been woven, those half-mythical artists whose real characters become cloaked for ever under a veil of the bizarre. They become known not as creatures of flesh and blood, living day by day as prosaically as the rest of us, but as men stepping on clouds, snaring a world of beauty from the trees and the sky, half wild, half human. It is, on the whole, a popular and an entertaining fallacy.

I recently found myself in Naples, in a small dim room in a huge Italian bank, gazing in awe at Caraveggio's last painting, completed just days before his tragic death. I leaned in a little too close to the canvas and set off the alarms and security poured in breaking the spell. When I left the room I was struck by a phrase about the artist from a near contemporary biography on an explanatory panel. Caraveggio, it stated bluntly, "had died badly, as indeed he had lived." I immediately thought how the same might be said of Dylan Thomas; and even more so when I saw that that Caraveggio had died, like Dylan, aged just 39.

*   *   *

Dylan's good friend and colleague, the Irish poet Louis MacNiece, had this to say after Dylan's death:

As for the "wild man" conception, immediately after Thomas's death it was exploited in its most disgusting and imbecilic form by certain of our daily papers. Of course Thomas liked pints of beer (so what? He also liked watching cricket) but he did not write his poems "with a pint in one hand"; no writer of our time approached his art in a more reverent spirit or gave it more devoted attention.

The great Welsh language poet and activist Saunders Lewis, in his obituary tribute to Dylan, reminds us that:

great creative powers are rarely unaccompanied by a devil-may-care extravagance. That was part of the genius of Dylan Thomas.

But the last words to to Augustus John, who figures largely in this book. This is the conclusion of his memoir of Dylan from his autobiography *Finishing Touches* (1964):

It was in New York that he broke down. It was there that whiskey, which he shunned in this country, played hell with his brain, with the dire results we know. And it was there that his poetic faculty deserted him completely, though he still did his stuff on the platform with tremendous success… The truth is that Dylan was at the core a typical Welsh puritan and nonconformist gone wrong. He was also a genius.

Dave Slivka's death mask of Dylan Thomas

Wales

WALES

Caitlin and Colm at the Laugharne St David's Day pageant

One of the reactions to Dylan Thomas's play for voices Under Milk Wood took an unexpected form. It was, I think, a group in Finland which proposed that missionaries should be sent to Wales to rescue its towns and villages from confusion and primitive horror. This would have delighted the poet even more than the praise which acclaimed his work. What tasks those missionaries would have to face! Dylan loved Wales, and he loved particularly Swansea, where he was born and wrote more than half his poems, and Laugharne, where his finest work in poetry and prose was finished, and where he lies buried.

– Vernon Watkins in the opening to his essay "The Wales Dylan Thomas Knew"

ADDRESSING A LITERARY AUDIENCE in Italy during his visit to the country for a few months in 1947, Dylan Thomas declared with his usual bombast:

One: I am a Welshman; two: I am a drunkard; three: I am a lover of the human race, especially of women.

It is worth noticing what comes first – Dylan Thomas is most proud to declare himself a Welshman. Later in his life he would introduce his readings in America with a preamble which stressed the effect Wales had had on his life and work;

I first saw the light and screamed at it in a loud lump of Wales… Naturally, my early poems and stories… came willy-nilly out of one particular atmosphere and environment, and are part and parcel, park and castle, lark and sea-shell, dark and school bell, muck and entrail, cock, rock and bubble, accent and sea-lap, root and rhythm of them.

He goes on to make one of his trademark, convoluted punning jokes about it:

If I had been born and brought up in an igloo and lived on whales not in it, about the same would be true, except that then it would have been extremely unlikely had I become a writer.

However, as with most of his opinions, one encounters the usual ambivalence, and prevarication. As early as 1933 he writes to Pamela Hansford Johnson, "I'm sick and this bloody country is killing me". A year later, and he is writing to a new literary friend, Stephen Spender, of his, "natural hatred of Wales". In 1945 he writes to David Tennant, the owner of London's Gargoyle Club, that he cannot wait to get away from "from mean green horsethieving Wales". By 1950, he is writing back to some American friends offering them reciprocal hospitality, but he does little to sell his country, which he describes as:

This arsehole of the universe.

It is, however, worth noting, that the phrase often used by Dylan's denigrators to substantiate accusations of his lack of patriotism:

The Land of my Fathers! My Fathers can keep it

was a phrase actually written by Dylan in his film script for the darkly gothic tale of a Welsh mining disaster *The Three Weird Sisters (1948)*. The lines are written for his obnoxious character Owen Morgan Vaughan, who shouts them out in a rage. Vaughan is a character light years away from Dylan Thomas. It is a sentiment which fits the film script but is not in any way being offered as Dylan's own opinion. According to Gwen Watkins, and other close friends, Dylan was indeed proud to be Welsh and although he was often frustrated by the parochialism and inwardness he encountered, he had a warm fondness for the:

strange Wales, coal-pitted, mountained, river run, full so far as I knew, of choirs and football teams and sheep and story-books, tall black hats and red flannel petticoats… that unknown Wales with its wild names like peals of bells in the darkness, and its mountain men clothed in the skins of animals perhaps and always singing'. (*Reminiscences of Childhood*, 1943*)*

Wales was a country littered with pubs, many of them the kind of pubs he loved to visit. However, he could also rejoice in their very nomenclature. Dylan had written early in his life of the profound effect the sound of words had on him:

I had fallen in love with words… What the words stood for, symbolised, or meant was of secondary importance; what mattered was the sound of them… words to me were as the notes of bells.

The mere names alone of the pubs of Wales were music to his ears:

the Mountain Sheep… the Blue Bull, the Dragon, The Star of Wales, the Twll in the Wall, the Sour Grapes, the Shepherd's Arms, the Bells of Aberdovey… the Druid's Tap: I had nothing to do in the whole wild August world but remember the names.

– from "The Outing"

Swansea

The basis of Dylan Thomas's work, in all its violent, teeming, comic, tragic, and exuberant imagination, is to be found in Swansea. From his parents' house at the top of Cwmdonkin Drive he projected his carefully constructed early poems over the roofs of the town; and Cwmdonkin Park.

– from Vernon Watkins's essay "The Wales Dylan Thomas Knew"

I was born in a large Welsh industrial town at the beginning of the Great War: an ugly lovely town (or so it was, and is, to me), crawling, sprawling, unplanned, jerryvilla'd and smug-suburbed by the side of a long and splendid-curving shore.

Sunny Swansea in 1934, the newly completed Guildhall is central, The Bay View Hotel to the right and a busy beach in the foreground

Thus opens the radio broadcast *Reminiscences of Childhood* (1943), with a typical love/hate statement. Writing for the local paper about George Borrow's *Wild Wales,* Dylan quotes Borrow's description of Swansea – "a large bustling dirty gloomy place" which is so very much like his own "ugly lovely town". Another of Dylan's favourite poets, Edward Thomas, had also preceded him in suggesting this dichotomy. Edward Thomas described his Swansea as encompassing both "Heaven and Hell" and he referred to it as being both a "horrible and sublime town". Some fifty years after Dylan's "ugly lovely" this phrase has yet again been brought up to date and transformed into the current patois. Local poet and artist Alan Perry wrote a short play set in Ralph the Books, the bookshop owned by Dylan's friend Ralph Wishart, where Dylan spent many happy browsing hours. In the play Alan coined the phrase "Pretty Shitty City" to describe his Swansea, which in turn became the opening motif for Kevin Allen's wonderfully scurrilous Swansea-based film *Twin Town* (1993).

At different times Swansea to Dylan, is "smug", "a dingy hell", "shabby" and "badly built", but at other times he writes of the town with real "hiraeth" (longing); to his Swansea friend Charlie Fisher –

Swansea is "still the best place". He pines:

to hear the sweet town accent float into (his) ears.

To Vernon Watkins he writes longingly:

I have nothing to do but wait for Swansea, marble-town, city of laughter, little Dublin, home of at least 2 great men.

And nowhere is his love of Swansea more evident than in his post-war radio play *Return Journey*, first broadcast in 1947. The premise of the play is that the older Dylan returns to his home town in search of his younger self. However his Swansea had recently been decimated by the horrendous Three Nights Blitz. The play opens with the narrator, the older Dylan, entering the bar (where else?) of Swansea's Station Hotel:

The bar was just opening but already one customer puffed and shook at the counter with a full pint of half frozen Tawe water in his wrapped up hand. The narrator orders a pint of bitter and asks the barmaid:
NARRATOR: I wonder if you remember a friend of mine? He always used to come to this bar some years ago, every morning about this time.
BARMAID: What's his name?
NARRATOR: Young Thomas.
BARMAID: Lots of Thomases come here it's a kind of home from home for Thomases… what's he look like?
NARRATOR: He'd be about seventeen or eighteen…
BARMAID: I was seventeen once.
NARRATOR: … and above medium height. Above medium height for Wales, I mean, he's five foot six-and-

a-half. Thick blubber lips; snub nose; curly mousebrown hair; one front tooth broken after playing a game called Cats and Dogs, in The Mermaid Mumbles; speaks rather fancy; truculent; plausible; a bit of a shower-off; plus fours and no breakfast, you know; used to have poems printed in the Herald of Wales… lived up the Uplands; a bombastic adolescent provincial bohemian with a thick-knotted tie made out of his sister's scarf… and a cricket shirt dyed bottle green; a gabbing, mock tough, pretentious young man; and mole-y, too.
BARMAID: There's words what d'you want to find him for I wouldn't touch him with a barge-pole.

But shortly another customer joins in:

I seem to remember a chap like you describe. There couldn't be two like him let's hope. He used to work as a reporter. Down The Three Lamps I used to see him. Lifting his ikkle elbow.

And after a walk down the High Street, where the narrator names every business, it is to The Three Lamps he goes, "that snug, smug, select Edwardian holy of best-bitter holies…" where "fair do's, they throw you out very genteel".

The play has a real warmth and nostalgia, but the devastation wrought by three terrible nights of relentless bombing raids gives it an underlying sadness. Dylan's friend Bert Trick recalls:

Dylan and I were to meet only once more. This was in 1941. It was the morning after the night of a devastating bombing attack on Swansea by the German Luftwaffe. Dylan, Caitlin and I met on the corner of Oxford Street, which overnight had become a black heaving ruin. The air was acrid with smoke and the hoses of the firemen snaked amongst the blackened entrails of what had once been Swansea market. As we parted, Dylan said with tears in his eyes – "Our Swansea is dead." No requiem was uttered more true or in fewer words.

Dead perhaps, but Dylan still gives the town a peculiar mention in *Under Milk Wood*, when blind Captain Cat is listening to the street kids playing below his window and he hears:

Billy Swansea with the dog's voice… Somebody's hit Maggie Richards. Two to one it's Billy Swansea. Never trust a boy who barks.

The critic and biographer John Ackerman sums up Dylan's time in Swansea:

At this time Dylan found that the pub was his natural background, the place to meet people and to talk and also to listen… The pub, too, provided the sounding board for his wit, was where good talk could flow as easily as the beer, and where opening hours provided easy, convivial company, pals ever ready to exchange the tall story, the ribald joke, the delightful item of news or gossip concerning the weird vagaries of human nature; and here, too, beery fantasy kept at bay the outside world.

The Uplands Hotel

Uplands Square

DYLAN THOMAS was born in the front bedroom of 5 Cwmdonkin Drive in the suburb of Swansea known as the Uplands on October 27th, 1914, and it would be his home for the first twenty years of his life. Whenever he wrote about the house it was always with an edge of slightly embarrassed disparagement:

> A mortgaged villa in an upper-class professional row. A small, not very well painted, gateless house... Very nice, very respectable.

Dylan's father, David John Thomas, was by 1914 established as head of English at the Swansea Grammar School and he had recently bought the new semi-detached house from the builder, in what was a fast developing, Swansea west, middle-class suburb. DJ proudly moved his pregnant wife Florrie, and eight-year-old daughter Nancy into the new semi shortly before Dylan's birth. Dylan would later christen himself as:

> Belly-churning Thomas, the Rimbaud of Cwmdonkin Drive.

Number Five was towards the top of a steep road overlooking the town and out to sea. It dropped down towards the cluster of shops and businesses, a cinema and churches, parks and pubs that made up the self-contained Uplands Square. Most of the locals' needs could be met here (the various shops in the square were quite by chance all named with colours – Mr Green the sweet shop, Mr Black the cobbler, Mr Gray the newsagent and Whites the shoe shop, and Dylan convinced his school pals that you could only open a business in Uplands if your name was a colour). All this was within walking distance of the town centre, the seafront, the rugby and cricket ground and the university.

Across the road was the delightful, Victorian, Cwmdonkin Park. This was the almost constant backdrop to Dylan's early years and it would later be celebrated in some of his greatest poems such as *The Hunchback in the Park* and *Should Lanterns Shine*, which ends:

> *The ball I threw while playing in the park*
> *Has not yet reached the ground.*

Dylan's autobiographical short stories *Portrait of the Artist as a Young Dog* (1940) contains one story "Patricia, Edith, and Arnold" which is set entirely in the park's magical landscape where his nanny left "footprints... as large as a horse's in the thickening snow" and young Dylan sledged across the "forbidden grass". When the boy is finally persuaded to leave the park for home he suddenly remembers:

I've left my cap by the snow man... It's my cap with the Tottenham colours.

I have never seen a reference to Dylan Thomas as a Spurs fan – surely if he were around today he would be writing praise-poems to the high-flying Premiership Swansea City FC!

At the age of seven, Dylan's world would shift down the hill to Mirador Crescent, an elegant terrace that curves around the back of Uplands Square and where Dylan was enrolled by his somewhat aspirational parents at Mrs Hole's private "Dame" school:

so firm and kind and smelling of goloshers.

Later, as he entered his teens, he began to develop his infatuation with films. He became a regular at the local "flea-pit" cinema on the corner of The Grove, a turning off the upper corner of the Square. These visits, plus extensive background reading, enabled him to contribute a quite precocious essay, "The Films", to his school magazine, which contains references to Griffith's Birth of a Nation and Zukor's Queen Elizabeth. It appeared in 1930 when Dylan was just 15. But soon, to these early haunts would be added the final stop-off, The Uplands Hotel, Dylan's first "local" and where he first began to love the pub. He would describe what he referred to as his "provincial rhythm" which included "one (or perhaps two) pints of beer in The Uplands Hotel."

In his letters he makes out that he visited this pub daily. For a while this was probably true and he continued to call in there when he later returned to Swansea, as his school friend Guido Heller describes:

One day I happened to be in Swansea in the Uplands, and who should I bump into but Dylan and Danny Jones together. It was after the war, yes – Dylan immediately said, "Right, we have to celebrate this meeting, we must go to the pub and have one"... while we were standing in the bar drinking, a dog walked across the bar, you see, a little brown terrier. So Dylan turned to me and said, "You know I do like a dog. But this particular dog has got to have a really nice brown arse." And he said, "There, look at that one, it's got it." And this was Dylan.

Dylan's deep love of this part of town – his "hiraeth" – is evident in the nostalgic letters he wrote to his Swansea friends after he left Swansea for London. In a letter to Dan Jones, sent from Ireland in 1935, just a year after leaving Swansea, Dylan is already wistfully dreaming of returning:

We must, when our affairs are settled, when our music and poetry are arranged so that we can still live, love, and drink beer, to go back to the Uplands... and found there, for good and for all, a permanent colony: living there until we are old gentlemen, with occasional visits to London and Paris, we shall lead the lives of a small town anti-society.

Sadly this was a dream that Dylan never managed to realise.

The Uplands Tavern today

This pub is now known as The Uplands Tavern, which is, at least, a huge improvement from the horrendous 1970s makeover which saw the interior totally gutted and Disney-fied, with faux booths, designed as mock shops, themed around Dylan Thomas, and the pub was renamed The Streets. Thankfully all this is now long gone. It is still a very a popular haunt, mainly with a rather louche ageing crowd of Swansea's more alternative inhabitants who cluster there on weekends for the line-up of local bands and musicians, and satisfies its location with a discreet corner bar decorated with recent paintings depicting scenes of Dylan's life.

In 2012 a new festival was launched in the Uplands, the Do Not Go Gentle Festival. It was designed to be the kind of festival that Dylan Thomas might have enjoyed and so it was – a heady mix of poetry music, drama and events at various Uplands venues including the Tavern. Held in November, the festival proved a popular success and is being planned as a new annual event in Swansea's arts calendar (www.donotgogentlefestival.com)

The Bay View Hotel

Oystermouth Road

THE BAY VIEW pub is a curious, tall and thin, wedge-shaped, flat-iron building on the corner of St Helens Road and Oystermouth Road, overlooking Swansea sands and across to the Mumbles Lighthouse. Today it seems an odd location for a large pub, set in a kind of no-man's land between Swansea city centre and Mumbles, but when it opened back in 1860, it was an important stop on the route of the Mumbles Railway that curved around the sweeping bay, which the Victorian poet Walter Savage Landor praised over and above the Bay of Naples. Back then this area of beach was, at least in the summer, a thriving holiday destination for locals and visitors.

The pub was built in 1859 and was originally supposed to be the centrepiece of a kind of mini Disney-like theme park, comprising the pub/hotel, surrounded by a sanatorium, a bowling green, billiard rooms, skating rink, pleasure gardens and a raised promenade where patrons could walk, sit up high and enjoy refreshment while gazing out at the panoramic sea views. But its position – neither in Swansea town nor in Oystermouth – proved to be its downfall and all

The Bay View and the Mumbles Train, circa 1915

that survived of the grandiose scheme was the pub. But early photographs show that the hotel and beach were a popular local destination.

Dylan Thomas describes in rich detail an August Bank Holiday he spent there in his radio script *Holiday Memory*, first broadcast in 1946. It consists of endless verbal renditions of Donald McGill-type saucy postcard images:

> August Bank Holiday. A tune on an ice-cream cornet. A slap of sea and a tickle of sand. A fanfare of sunshades opening. A wince and whinny of bathers dancing into the deceptive water. A tuck of dresses. A rolling of trousers. A compromise of paddlers. A sunburn of girls and a lark of boys. A silent hullabaloo of balloons... And trams that hissed liked ganders took us all to the beautiful beach. There was cricket on the sand, and sand in the sponge cake, sand-flies in the watercress and foolish, mulish, religious donkeys on the unwilling trot. Girls undressed in slipping tents of propriety... Little navvies dug canals... wispy young men, outside bathing huts, whistled

at substantial women... Recalcitrant uncles huddled over luke-warm ale in tiger striped marquees... In the distance, surrounded by disappointed theoreticians and an ironmonger with a drum, a man on an orange box shouted that holidays were wrong.

It is interesting to note that Gwen Watkins writes of Dylan:

> spending a whole evening with Vernon and Alfred Janes, reading and discussing the first draft of his Bank Holiday script, on a single bottle of beer.

Dylan was obviously a fan of the area, and he uses it to great advantage in two of his stories in *Portrait of The Artist as a Young Dog*. In "One Warm Saturday", Dylan's favourite from this collection, The Bay View is thinly disguised as The Victoria, situated – as it is in reality – just along from Victoria Gardens, with its "flower clock" and "white-tiled urinal". Dylan describes the scene in the rich descriptive prose he would later use in his *Holiday Memory* broadcast. The story opens with his main character, Jack (Dylan himself), sat near "The Bay View":

> a young man in a sailor's jersey, sitting near the summer huts to see the brown and white women coming out and the groups of pretty-faced girls with pale vees and scorched backs.

The boy joins in with a family's impromptu game of cricket, played with a tin tray for a bat, and then listens in to a:

hell-fire preacher on a box marked Mr Matthews [who] shook his cold hands, stormed at the holiday, and cursed the summer from his shivering box.

This preacher also appears in "Old Garbo", where he is described as a "neat man" who "held his banner high and prominently feared the Lord", and again in *Holiday Memory* he is "a cross man on an orange box" who "shouted that holidays were wrong". He morphs over the years into *Under Milk Wood*'s mad Jack Black the cobbler, who has his trouser fly buttons sewn up to deter the sin of Onan, and chases:

> the naughty couples down the grassgreen gooseberried bed of the wood... [screaming] Ach y fi! Ach y fi! ...Off to Gomorah!

Our hero then enters the pub in order to drown his sorrows, having failed to have summoned up the courage to engage with a young girl, Lou, who he had sat beside on a bench near the flower gardens. In his disappointment and confusion he refers to her as both "the girl in a million" but in the next breath as "a queer tart in a park". He sees himself reflected in the pub mirror and ruminates:

> And what shall the terrified prig of a love-mad young man do next? He asked his reflection in the distorting mirror of the empty Victoria saloon. His ape like hanging face, with "Bass" across his forehead, gave back a cracked sneer. But soon he is drinking with an archetypal barman, "I like them big myself. Once round Bessy, once round the gasworks. I missed the chance of a lifetime, too. Fifty lovelies in the nude and I'd left my Bunsen burner at home".

Before long his lost girl enters the pub with a couple of brassy friends. Dylan gets drawn into their company and their racy talk, in which even Mr Matthews gets at least some support when one of the other "ladies" ventures;

> But there's a lot in what the preacher says, mind, about carrying on. If you go for a constitutional after stop-tap along the sands you might as well be in Sodom and Gomorrah.

The lad ends up going on to a rather sordid party with his dream girl, her friends and a group of assorted no-good-boyos picked up in the pub. But it all ends sadly when Jack tries to find a lavatory and then, sadly and frustratingly, cannot find his way back to Lou's room. He leaves dejected for "no bed but his own too many miles away" in a town full of "never-to-be-forgotten people" who had:

> lived and loved and died and, always, lost.

The other *Portrait* story set around The Bay View is "Just Like Little Dogs". Again the young narrator (Dylan himself) is out at night, loitering under one of the railway arches near to the pub, sheltering from the cold wind and rain and considering his lot:

> There was no sense in standing silent for hours under a railway arch on a hell of a night at the end of a summer when girls were waiting, ready to be hot and friendly, in chip shops and shop doorways and Rabbiotti's all-night café, when the public bar of The Bay View at the corner, had a fire and skittles and a swarthy, sensuous girl with different coloured eyes.

It is interesting to note that what the narrator desires of the pub is the warmth of the fire, the fun of the skittle alley and the conviviality and the ocular beauty of the "sensuous girl" – and that he makes no mention of drink at all. He is joined under the arch by two men – Tom and Walter, and they eventually regale him with a detailed account of a night spent with two girls, Doris and Norma. It began as a "story-telling thing in the arch", but then "gave place to the loving night in the dunes", which, in turn, led to paternity suits. It ends with them in court, during which the old judge vehemently describes them as behaving, "just like little dogs". However they end up marrying their respective partners:

> We had to do the right thing by them, didn't we?

And our forlorn narrator is left considering his evening:

> All at once I remembered how cold I was . I rubbed my numb hands together. Fancy standing all night in the cold. Fancy listening, I thought, to a long, unsatisfactory story in the frost-bite in a polar arch.

Apart from these two fictionalised accounts of The Bay View we also have an account of Dylan and his good friend Vernon Watkins starting Dylan's twenty-second birthday celebrations in the pub. In her book on the two poets *Portrait of a Friend*, Gwen Watkins gives us a detailed account of the evening's proceedings which begins:

They started off with a drink at The Bay View Hotel, then took turns to ride Vernon's bicycle along the Mumbles Road to Oystermouth, ending up at Dylan's favourite pub, The Mermaid.

But you can read more of this escapade in the pages about The Mermaid!

The Bay View today

The Bay View is a thriving pub/restaurant with a reputation for good Thai food and live music. And thankfully the twee "e" which was once added to "Bay" has been rightfully discarded! And even more thankfully the brewery owners' scheme to re-brand all their pubs as alliterative "Firkin" pubs, which saw The Bay View renamed The Foreshore and Firkin, was also seen as a marketing error and The Bay View lives on with its original and best name intact.

The Three Lamps

Castle Square, Swansea (renamed The Office)

WHEN DYLAN left school, aged 17, with just one successful exam result (in English), his father got him a job as a trainee on the local paper ("Daddy thought it would be a good opening for him," said Mrs Thomas). Dylan spent about 18 months on the *Daily Post* as it was then, learning little about journalism but much about pub culture and "manly drinking". In his radio play *Return Journey*, his hymn of "hiraeth" for his bombed, blitzed and beloved Swansea, he recalls some of his old colleagues who used to meet in The Three Lamps:

> And into Temple St. There had stood, old Mac magisterial in his corner and there the young Thomas who I was searching for used to stand at the counter on Friday pay night with Freddie Farr Half Hook, Bill Latham, Cliff Williams, Gareth Hughes, Eric Hughes and Glyn Lowery. A man among men, in that snug, smug, elect Edwardian holy of best bitter holies.

Of these old hacks, Dylan's chief mentor was senior reporter Freddie 'Half Hook' Farr who features

. the threat of the clutched tankard

in Dylan's earlier short story "Old Garbo" published in *Portrait of the Artist as a Young Dog*. It is from these autobiographical stories that we learn so much about Dylan's rite of passage through Swansea's more colourful public houses. It is an account of his first real Swansea pub crawl under the tutelage of Freddie Farr, who, after a day's work, abruptly orders young Dylan to meet him:

> Six o'clock in The Lamps back bar.

The Three Lamps was then situated in Temple Street just across the road from the *Daily Post* offices which nestled into the ruins of Swansea Castle. It was a bar favoured by Swansea's professional men and it would become a favourite pub of Dylan's. With these real seasoned drinking companions, Dylan feels he is attaining true manhood and wishes his father could see him as he takes his place at the bar:

> The back bar of The Three Lamps was full of elderly men. Mr Farr had not yet arrived. I leant against the bar, between an alderman and a solicitor, drinking bitter, wishing that my father could see me now… He could not fail to see that I was a boy no longer, nor fail to be angry at the angle of my fag and my hat and the threat of the clutched tankard.

He continues with a majestic and poetic hymn to the glories of beer:

> I liked the taste of beer, its live white lather, its brass bright depths, the sudden world through the wet brown walls of the glass, the tilted rush to the lips and the slow swallowing

down to the lapping belly, the salt on the tongue, the foam at the corners.

Old Mr Farr, however, has seen it all before:

> Mr Farr sneered down his glass as I watched the young men enviously and saw how much she (the pretty barmaid) liked their ways, how she slapped their hands lightly and wriggled back, in pride of her prettiness and gaiety to pull the beer-handles. "Toop little Twms from the Valleys. There'll be some puking to-night," he said, with pleasure.

This last sentence is an uncommon example of Dylan using vernacular Welsh – "toop" is his phonetic rendition of the Welsh "twp" meaning simple or daft and "Twms" is "Toms" in English, but here it is a somewhat derogatory Welsh word for country bumpkins. There has been much debate among scholars as to just how much Welsh Dylan knew and used. Since both his parents were Welsh speakers and his relatives in Carmarthen would have used Welsh as their first language, it is inconceivable that Dylan could not have acquired some Welsh – even if inadvertently, by some kind of osmosis.

Another of his colleagues on the *Post*, Bill Latham, describes the pub in his unpublished memoir:

> The Three Lamps had a character of its own because the landlord (Old Mac) sat in the corner and controlled proceedings, and he would be very offended if anyone even held up his glass of beer to the light, to allege that it was cloudy or anything of that sort… it frequently means that several other people hold their glass up to the light too, and people begin to think "is there something wrong with this beer or isn't

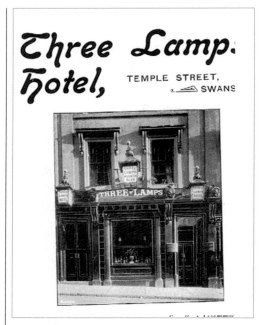

The original Three Lamps

there?" And the very sight of one man holding his glass up was enough to send Mac into a complete rage… Dylan sometimes held his glass up deliberately to provoke him!

This reinforces just how beer was venerated and respected and one can see how it provoked Dylan's hymn to its glories. And it also offers a prime example of the childish, mischievous behaviour that Dylan would never lose. But perhaps the last words on this pub should come from *Return Journey*. In the opening scene in a High Street pub, the narrator engages with a local man, who recalls seeing:

The magnificent, original Ben Evans department store

The devastated centre of Swansea after the air raids

a chap like you described. There couldn't be two like him let's hope. He used to work as a reporter. Down The Three Lamps I used to see him. Lifting his ikkle elbow.

In *Return Journey* we learn the sad fate of the original Three Lamps, when the narrator asks a local what it is like now:

"It isn't like anything. It isn't there. It's nothing mun. You remember Ben Evans Stores? It's right next door to that. Ben Evans isn't there either."

Sadly, the whole area was levelled to the ground during the Three Nights Blitz.

The Three Lamps after its Sixties rebuild and relocation but before it was renamed The Office, but why it was considered an improvement on the original name – or any sort of an inviting name for a pub – is beyond me

The Three Lamps today

Today the new pub fronts onto the newly refurbished Castle Square where the central feature is a fine stone and glass sculptural fountain by a world renowned local artist, Amber Hiscott. The glass leaf which rests on top of the fountain is inspired by lines from one of Dylan's early notebook poems "Rain cuts the place we tread". Written when he was just 16, it contains the lines:

> We sail a boat upon the path:
> Paddle with leaves
> Down an ecstatic line of light.

Across the road from the pub are the ruins of the old Swansea Castle. Back in Dylan's day the offices of the *South Wales Daily Post*, where Dylan started work, were nestled alongside the castle walls. After the pub's devastation during The Blitz it was rebuilt close to its original site and it is still there but has been gruesomely renamed as The Office. Go in for a drink if you will, but take a paperback copy of Dylan's short stories, read "Old Garbo" and use your imagination to the full!

Inside, the current pub has a central bar with seating all around. There is a large stage at the front and when there is no band playing, tables and chairs give a great view over the fountain, which is lit up at night.

The No Sign Bar

Wind Street

T HIS FAMOUS, but easy-to-miss establishment, has the smallest frontage of any pub in Swansea, and is situated on Wind Street, (pronounced Wine Street), in what was once the business and commercial centre of the town. Local folklore has it that the street was named thus because it was once home to many Swansea wine-merchants, but the Welsh version of the name "Stryd y Gwynt" would suggest that the long narrow street was once a gusty blow-hole of a place and is named for purely meterological reasons. However at least one wine business, The No Sign Wine Bar, run by a Swansea wine-dealing dynasty, the Munday family, has played its part in the street's history for more than 300 years.

The first reference to a "no custom house" can be found in a document of 1690. This ancient building has been licensed throughout its recorded history, being in turn brew house, brewery, wine and spirits merchants and public house. It appears to have been overlooked at the time when licensing was introduced and when every public house had to have a sign by which it could be recognised (which is why two public houses of the same name are never found in the same vicinity). It appears that number 56, which in those days was a 'bar' not a 'house', was not allocated its own sign. When this oversight was recognised, the early bureaucratic error was rectified by giving the establishment its curious name. In the twentieth century the interior became something of a museum to the wine trade with large old oil paintings of gentleman connoisseurs and vintners, and grand glazed cabinets containing vintage bottles and wine-making paraphernalia. Until quite recently it did only sell wine and spirits – no beers were offered.

As Dylan was almost exclusively a beer drinker in his Swansea days, it may not have been one of his regular haunts, but if it lacked ale it made up for it with a wonderful antiquarian atmosphere, and as it was just down the road from his Swansea workplace at the *Daily Post*, he no doubt had occasion to call in. His good friend Mabley remembers often visiting:

> Mundays Wine Shop opposite the Post Office… a little bar where you sit surrounded by enormous barrels, vast quantities of bottles, completely cut-off from the world outside. Where time seems to stop… you could sit for hours without being conscious of being part of the world and surrounded by all the atmosphere and apparatus of drink.

The bar is almost right on the corner of a wonderful (well wonderfully named at least), pedestrian alleyway which rejoices in the name of Salubrious Passage. It is often given the sobriquet "Dickensian" and back in the 80s I was so pleased to locate my bookshop there – what an address for an "olde-worlde" rare bookshop. Sadly, as the banks and offices on Wind Street all became giant ugly pub after pub, and the area turned into an infamous binge-drinking hotspot, our bookshop became anachronistic and we relocated to a more bookish area. We did call our new premises Salubrious House – it was just too good a name to lose!

High up above Wind Street and Salubrious Passage, on the top floor of the corner building, one of Dylan's good friends had a workshop. Alban Leyshon was something of a local legend and a fringe member of Dylan's Kardomah gang. A gifted but eccentric craftsman and jewellery maker, he was also something of an inventor. Alban is said to have designed and crafted a gold ring for the snooker wizard Joe Davies, which was shaped as a billiard table complete with semi-precious stones for the balls. Dylan is said to have called up to see Alban and, somewhat sadistically, amused himself by using Alban's Bunsen burner to heat pennies until they were red hot. Then he would carefully throw them out the window and laugh cruelly as unsuspecting pedestrians heard the clink, and grabbed at the coins, and burned their fingers!

Alban's fame as a mad-scientist/eccentric inventor even made it to pages of no less a journal than *Life* magazine, in this article from the issue for November 24th, 1952.

Alban Leyshon proves the strength of his 'hollow bricks' for Life *magazine*

The bar and the passageway made enough of an impression on Dylan that some twenty years later he locates his only ghost story, "The Followers", in this part of Swansea. It would appear, however, that Dylan found Salubrious Passage along with The No Sign Bar just too Dylanesque and in his story he renames them. Salubrious Passage becomes Paradise Alley and The

No Sign Bar becomes The Vaults. It is interesting to note that this story was not written until the last year of Dylan's life. It appeared in the periodical *World Review* in October 1953, just weeks before Dylan died, and yet the story harks back to his youthful days pubbing in his home town. The story begins with a series of vignettes of the people of Swansea on a wet weekday evening:

> A flat long girl drifted snivelling into her hanky, out of a jeweller's shop… She looked, in the grey rain, as though she were crying from top to toe.
>
> A man with a balloon tied to his hat pushed a shrouded barrow up a dead end.
>
> A baby with an ancient face sat in its pram outside the Wine Vaults, quiet, very wet, peering cautiously round.

The narrator meets his pal Leslie, and they exchange some boasting sexual banter:

> A plump blonde girl, smelling of wet rabbits, self-conscious even in the dirty night, minced past on high-heeled shoes. The heels clicked, the soles squelched. Leslie whistled after her, low and admiring.
>
> "Business first," I said.
>
> "Oh, boy!" Leslie said.
>
> "And she's too fat as well."
>
> "I like them corpulent," Leslie said. "Remember Penelope Bogan? A Mrs too."
>
> "Oh come on. That old bird of Paradise Alley!"

The story would suggest that Dylan's nostalgia for Swansea is by no means all rose-tinted. His detailed

My "Dylans Bookstore" was once proudly based in Salubrious Passage

description of a fictional local, The Marlborough, is far from complimentary. He shows contempt for the officialdom that has appeared on the walls of the pub and his character announces his plan to subvert the pub's over-the-top restrictive code of behaviour:

> The Marlborough saloon was cold and empty. There were notices on the damp walls: "No Singing. No Dancing. No Gambling. No Peddlers."
>
> "You sing," I said to Leslie, "and I'll dance, then we'll have a game of nap and I'll peddle my braces."

He goes on to describe this imagined pub and he seems to have become somewhat disenchanted with the place:

> The peeling, liver-coloured room might never have been drunk in at all. Here, commercials told jokes and had Scotches and sodas with happy, dyed, port-and-lemon women; dejected regulars grew grand and muzzy in the corners… reprobate grannies in dustbin black cackled and nipped; influential nobodies revised the earth; a party, with earrings, called "Frilly Willy" played the crippled piano, which sounded like a hurdy-gurdy playing underwater, until the publican's nosy wife said, "No". Strangers came and went, but mostly went. Men from the valleys dropped in for nine or ten; sometimes there were fights; and always there was something doing, some argie-bargie, giggle and bluster, horror or folly, affection, explosion, nonsense, peace, some wild goose flying in the boozy air of that comfortless, humdrum nowhere in the dizzy, ditchwater town at the end of the railway lines. But that evening it was the saddest room I had ever known.

This, written in the last year of his life, suggests that Dylan's love affair with the pub was waning.

The No Sign Wine Bar today

Today the No Sign is thriving as a rare independent bar surrounded by tasteless, giant themed chain pubs. The front bar is still largely unspoilt and homely, with coal fires in the winter and bare wooden floors, offering good beers, wines and spirits. But its back bars and commodious cellars now offer a variety of culinary and musical treats. I am sure it is the only bar on Wind Street in which Dylan would still be happy to take a drop!

The No. 10

Union Street, Swansea

THE NO. 10 was a distinctive looking pub with a fine mock-Tudor timbered frontage with a curious hanging, glazed lamp decorated with a devilish imp and the words "Ye Olde Wine Shoppe". But it was more famous for what greeted and astounded customers on entering. The pub boasted and hosted a large stuffed and somewhat fearsome Bavarian bear! Such an accessory was bound to appeal to Dylan's surrealistic bent. The folklore surrounding this curiosity is dense and varied. Was he affectionately known as Archie or Boris? Was he left behind alive by a touring circus in the late nineteenth or early years of the twentieth century? Or was he the stuffed remains of a dancing bear that performed around Swansea town? This dancing bear is at least recorded in print in a book published in 1866. *Reminiscences of Old Swansea* records:

> my recollection of having seen some men with a dancing bear exhibiting on the open field where Lower Oxford Street now is, to a small crowd of bystanders.

The bear was a favourite of another famous son of Swansea, the Goon Show comedian and singer Harry Secombe, who talked of his love for the "stuffed bear at The No. 10", and film star Peter Sellers, and co-Goon, was photographed next to it while filming *Only Two Can Play* in Swansea in 1962. An even more bizarre story has rock guitar legend Jimi Hendrix visiting Swansea in the 60s to listen to local bands and having his photo taken beside the great bear. A former No. 10 regular recalled: "the photograph, which showed Jimi Hendrix smoking a dubious cigarette with his arm around Boris, appeared in a number of magazines at the time".

Boris/Archie became the centre of a number of alcohol-related pranks – often showered with beer by inebriated customers and kidnapped on a number of occasions only to be discovered later at various locations around Swansea. Dylan used the pub as a regular and arranged to meet his friend Vernon Watkins there when he was staying with his parents in Bishopston in May of 1940. The meeting never happened as this letter reveals:

> Dear Vernon:
> The first word since the death of our date in the No. 10… what a pity we never could arrange longer and noisier evenings: noisy with our own poems.

Dylan locates the opening of his *Portrait of the Artist…* story "The Peaches" in Union Street and has the young Dylan left "late on an April evening" on his uncle Jim's cart outside a pub, here called The Pure Drop, which could well be The No. 10. His uncle disappears inside, telling his young companion:

> I won't be two minutes… I'll be out straight away… you stay there quiet.

Young Dylan gets lonely, bored and scared, sitting in the road, trying to "see into half of a smoky, secret room", and he is soon imagining the worst:

> a man with spring-heeled boots and a two-edged knife might be bouncing towards me from Union Street.

The young lad then climbs down and goes to sleep under a bench outside the pub. After his pit-stop Uncle Jim comes out of the pub full of "rich noise and comfortable smells" and:

> backed the mare into Union Street, lurching against her side, cursing her patience and patting her nose, and we both climbed into the cart. "There are too many drunken gipsies," he said as we rolled and rattled through the flickering lamp-lit town… Off to the warmth and comfort of Aunt Annie's farm.

The Number 10 today

It is a rather pleasing irony that the building is no longer a pub, but is now an up-market health-food shop. The mock Tudor frontage and decorative lamp are still in place, but the beer and the bear have gone, and instead of ale and spirits all that can be bought is Sanatogen, ginseng and herbal health remedies.

Back in Dylan's day Union Street also boasted an establishment known as "Dirty Black's", which was owned and run by "Dirty Black the Fancy Man" and his wife. It sold novelties and jokes, but inside you could also buy contraceptives, which were still considered clandestine, and not readily available in those days. Dylan writes in his short story "Old Garbo" of looking in through the window of the shop:

> but it was innocent; there were only itching and sneezing powders, stink bombs, rubber pens and Charlie masks; all the novelties were inside.

but Dylan

> dared not go in for fear a woman serve me, Mrs Dirty Black with a moustache and knowing eyes, or a thin dog-faced girl I saw there once who winked and smelled of seaweed

While on the subject of contraceptives, I am reminded of a time when I was standing outside my bookshop when it was situated in Salubrious Passage. An old gent stopped to pass the time of day. He began to reminisce about a barber who had worked in what became my bookshop, but some 60 years earlier. He was known as "The Great Vitoski", a real character who told stories of cutting the hair of the great and the good (and the bad) on Broadway, New York. In Swansea he barbered and shaved the seamen when they came up from the docks – his trick was a number of pre-made signs in a group of relevant languages. If a Russian ship was in dock the sign posted in the window would be in Russian declaring "Russian spoken here"; if it was a Spanish vessel up would go a sign, this time in Spanish, announcing "Spanish spoken here" – when in fact all the not-so great Vitoski spoke was a limited pidgin English, but he pulled in the punters!

The old boy told me all sorts of stories about Vitoski but his rheumy old eyes lit up again when he delighted in telling me that it was the first place in Swansea that you could get "them French letters!" The joy in his face showed that the memory obviously took him back to his more sexually active youth, but it pleased me that the building and my business was continuing to trade in letters, albeit of a rather different kind!

Remarkably the bear, at least, may still exist, now sadly and slowly disintegrating in the corner of another of Dylan's Swansea pubs – The Queens, where a stuffed bear is on display but it is a very sorry, hideously rotting example of the taxidermist's art and the jury is out on whether it is the original Archie/Boris – Swansea's amazing dancing bear!

The Queens Hotel

Swansea Maritime Quarter

THE QUEENS HOTEL is situated on the corner of Burrows Place and Cambrian Place, in what is now Swansea's gentrified Maritime Quarter, but at the start of the nineteenth century it was the centre of Swansea's docks area, and would have been full of seamen from all corners of the world. At that time these docks made Swansea the second busiest port in the UK, after Liverpool. The Queens is a building of great character, surrounded by elegant Georgian terraces, where wealthy ship owners and sea captains lived, and where all the major shipping companies had their offices. But alongside this elegance were the rough pubs and dives that the seafarers flocked to once they had docked, and Dylan became deeply captivated by this area.

A map, dated 1880, indicates that back then there were 14 pubs and licensed hotels in the area but today The Queens is the last survivor – and even this great old pub closed for a while in 1973. Dylan Thomas does not refer to this pub directly by name in any of his stories or letters, but during his time

as a young cub reporter, he was drawn down Wind Street and into this notorious area. It was one of the pubs conjured up in his story, "Old Garbo", when he writes of how, watching a boring film, his mind wanders and he dreams of:

the bob women and the pansy sailors in the dives.

Dylan writes about many pubs, some with imagined names, and others actual pubs, but long gone – The Bugle, The Jews Harp, The Fishguard Arms, The Heart's Delight, The Lord Nelson; names that evoked the spirit of these wild places which so fascinated Dylan.

Perhaps the most famous of these lost dockside pubs was The Cuba, which was destroyed in The Blitz. Its name is a testament to Swansea's rich association with the Caribbean through its involvement with the copper ore trade. The local papers at the turn of the century often carried accounts of violent clashes between the Cuba "girls" and the "young ladies" from The Queens. It would appear that each group believed in strict territorial demarcation lines, and fist fights would break out over transgressions and stolen customers – for both pubs were used by Swansea's busy streetwalkers.

The last landlady of The Cuba, Jean Cobley, remembers a particular regular – a sailor known to all as Happy Days. How Dylan would have loved Happy Days – and who knows maybe they did share a drink! Mrs Cobley recalls how, whenever Happy came ashore, he would hand his pay packet, a thick wad of dirty notes, over the bar to her husband

The Cuba Hotel, sadly destroyed in the Blitz

Glyn. He would then order his favourite tipple – a pint of spirits made up of a shot from each and every optic! – and then he would happily and inevitably slump into a corner at the end of the night, happy in the knowledge that his next few nights' drinking was paid for. The phrase "Happy Days" has become a Swansea-ism much used by current no-good boyos as a catch-all phrase for when things are going better than average on all fronts, or one in particular.

Another local character who would also have appealed to Dylan's love of the bizarre and unusual was Jerry the One-Legged Rigger. He has entered into local folklore and has even been celebrated in a sea shanty, the chorus of which goes:

Oh you may have a dock where you float round the clock,
And your ships may be faster and bigger,
But there's one thing we've got, which we're sure that
  you've not:
That's Jerry the one-legged rigger.

© Andrew McKay

Elements of all these vanished or imagined pubs are represented by The Queens. Dylan enjoyed and wrote about these lively and colourful pubs, and he would have been more than a little interested in the colourful women who could be found in and around the pubs too, for this area, with its crowds of lonely sailor boys, their pay packets burning holes in their pockets, was the hub of Swansea's red-light zone. To put it in no uncertain terms, The Queens was also a brothel!

Some "trade" was actually carried on in rooms in the pub – but that was for the better class of girl and better class of customer – the officers and captains. Regular seaman had to make do with a dark and dank area just along from the pub, in front of Swansea Museum – The Royal Institution of South Wales, and the oldest museum in the principality. Dylan refers to it in *Return Journey* as "the museum that should be in a museum". The rougher girls would ply their trade on the steps of this austere building. In "Just Like Little Dogs", Dylan describes the area as a place where:

methylated-spirit drinkers danced into policemen's arms and women like lumps of clothes in a pool waited, in doorways and holes in the soaking wall for vampires and firemen.

He goes on to describe the:

bad, ragged women who'd pretend against the museum wall for a cup of tea.

And in his story "One Warm Saturday", a pretentious but "tarty" woman, Mrs Emerald Franklyn – "dressed and made up to look young", is complaining vociferously about the "carrying on… after stop-tap along the sands… you might as well be in Sodom and Gomorrah". She is brought down to earth by her companion:

the blonde girl laughed. "Hark to Mrs Grundy! I see her with a black man last Wednesday, round by the museum".

But Emerald defends her honour:

He was Indian, from the University College, and I'd thank you to remember it. Everyone's brothers under the skin but there's no tarbrush in my family.

There is a story, told often enough to be true, that the ladies of the night would sit at the bar of The Queens, their feet on the brass footrest, with their

One of the Queen's "ladies" with her price list on the soles of her shoes

price list/menu writ large on the soles of their vampy shoes! And they used the chalk from the dartboard to write with! A brief lift of the foot was all that was needed to inform potential customers of the going rate for the particular forms of companionship on offer.

Also in "Old Garbo", the young and naive Dylan is promised pubs on the docks where he would see "sailors knitting there in the public bar" alongside "shilling women". When they enter the Fishguard:

> a man… slid out in front of us with a bottle or a black-jack in one gloved hand.

Young Dylan once more "wished they could have seen me now, in the dark, stunted room, with photographs of boxers peeling on the wall". And nearby was The Missions to Seamen Institute on Harbour Road, where:

> there might be a quarrel with razors.

And as evidence we learn the grisly fact that Ted Williams had once:

> found a lip outside The Mission to Seamen. It had a small moustache.

Just how much this Swansea street-life inspired the young writer is indicated at the start of "Old Garbo" when Dylan offers his readers a rich panoramic description of an average Saturday morning:

> junior clerks and shop assistants… Valley men… the country shoppers, the window gazers, the silent shabby men… the press of mothers… old women in black… smart girls… little dandy lascars… business men.

How he must have loved being able to juxtapose "dandy lascars" with "business men". Dylan ends the passage by declaring:

> I'll put you all in a story by and by.

"Old Garbo" does end with Dylan showing just such a story to his older mentor:

When I showed this story a long time later to Mr Farr, he said: "You got it all wrong. You got the people mixed. The boy with the handkerchief danced in the Jersey. Fred Jones was singing in the Fishguard. Never mind. Come and have one tonight in the Nelson. There's a girl down there who'll show you where a sailor bit her. And there's a policeman who knew Jack Johnson."

And Dylan ends by saying again, "I'll put them all in a story by and by".

One of Dylan's better biographers and critics, the Maesteg-born John Ackerman, observed this in an article on Dylan's prose:

> During the thirties Dylan Thomas was becoming a connoisseur of pub life, both in Swansea, Laugharne and London… and no doubt collecting those anecdotes and snippets of heard and overheard conversation that were to salt his prose comedy.

But back to The Queens – suffice to say any prostitution in this gentrified area of Swansea Marina is strictly a thing of the long distant past!

The Queens today

In The Queens today the walls of the pub are adorned with a fine collection of old, original maritime photographs of life as it once was in the Port of Swansea. The pub is now nominated by Camra for its real ales and draught beers. The Queens Hotel guarantees a warm welcome and is a must for all lovers of a traditional pub serving good beer and wholesome Welsh food. The *Lonely Planet Guide* sums it up succinctly: "An old-fashioned corner pub with polished mahogany and brass bar, old tiles and a range of cask-conditioned beers on tap, including Theakston's Old Peculier."

But be warned, although the current landlord, Gary Owens, is very welcoming, his doorman, in the form of a somewhat ravaged and disintegrating ten foot tall stuffed bear, is less so! I would welcome his final demise for – like the beer Gary sells – this bear is both very old and very peculiar.

Today this area is full of much more salubrious attractions. Just along the road is the current location of Swansea Little Theatre Group, in the recently refurbished Dylan Thomas Theatre, named after their most famous alumnus.

The building is decorated with a fine mural depicting the poet himself surrounded by characters from *Under Milk Wood*. The theatre fronts on to what is now known as Dylan Thomas Square which has an

The poet sits in a wooden chair; the chair is a fine likeness

imposing bronze statue of the seated poet, although some critics have questioned the accuracy of the likeness. When the statue was unveiled, Dylan's friend Dr Daniel Jones wrote a tongue-in-cheek letter to the local paper asking why Swansea should have a statue of the American singer Harry Belafonte on its dockside. Another Dylan scholar, James A Davies, wrote of it, with gentle, but pointed irony:

> And across the footbridge the Maritime Quarter has one more Dylan-inspired statue, this time of Captain Cat, the retired blind sea captain from Under Milk Wood. If you look closely at the buttons on the blind captain's reefer coat you will see they are lettered "I love you Rosie Probert". This was the sculptor Robert Thomas's clever way of making visible the hidden words tattooed on Captain Cat's belly.

Within a short walk of the pub you can visit a number of other interesting attractions. We have already mentioned Swansea Museum, but a short walk towards the marina will bring you to the National Industrial and Maritime Museum which was opened in 2000. Also nearby is the Dylan Thomas Centre with its permanent exhibition based on the Dylans Bookstore Collection of books, manuscripts, paintings and ephemera by and about Dylan.

You can add to this three good small art galleries – the Nick Holly Studio Gallery, the Attic Gallery and the Mission Gallery, which hosts contemporary art, painting, installation, photography and craft. It was formerly St Nicholas Church for seamen, and was designed by Benjamin Bucknall and built in 1886. Just eastward from The Queens are the modern offices of

the *South Wales Evening Post*, the paper then known as the *South Wales Daily Post* which once employed the young Dylan. Just further on again is one of Swansea's best hotels – Morgans – which was recently developed out of the fine old Port Authority building.

The Bush Inn

High Street Swansea

B Y A STRANGE and somewhat ironic coincidence the landlord of The Bush at around the time of Dylan's birth shared his father's name, D J Thomas, but perhaps that is not so strange in a town described by a character in Dylan's radio play, *Return Journey*, as being "a home from home for Thomases". The Bush, once a fine Georgian building (it is still grade II listed), has had a long history as one of the most important meeting places and stopovers in Swansea, and it is one of the few local inns to have been celebrated with its very own published history.

This rare and charming little book by W H Jones, who wrote numerous books on Swansea's history, was published in 1915 but it takes us as far back as the middle of the seventeenth century when The Bush Inn welcomed guests of immense importance. In 1655 Oliver Cromwell had created local hero Colonel Phillip Jones, High Steward of Swansea for "his activity in raising and directing the Parliamentarian Forces in Swansea and Glamorgan". Colonel Jones lived very close to The Bush Inn, and when Cromwell visited the town in 1648, and again in 1649, the

The Story of the Bush Inn AT SWANSEA — Proprietor - E. J. THOMAS

booklet informs us that he stayed with his soldier friend, and that "there is no reason to doubt that The Bush Inn participated in the high entertainment, which was lavishly bestowed upon Cromwell and his staff".

The author continues his narrative with tales of elaborate wagers and heavy betting – in 1804 the lively landlord William Jones accepted a bet:

A dozen cases of wine for the good of the house that Mr Jones does not walk thrice round the Burrows in thirteen minutes.

Such was the excitement engendered that the result appeared in the *Cambrian* newspaper:

Running and walking matches are becoming as much a rage here as in other places; two bets were decided on Christmas eve; Mr Jones of the Bush-inn was allowed 13 minutes to walk thrice round our Burrows, which he performed in twelve.

But we also learn that the distance involved was "little over a mile", that "our host was of portly build" and that being Christmas Eve:

the parties to the bet broached their wine and mine host made merry at other's expense.

EXTERIOR

Under William Jones the Bush developed a ballroom much loved by the local "fair-sex" and grand dances were held especially around Race Week when Swansea's Crymlyn Burrows became a veritable Aintree. The week culminated with a grand "Summer Ball at the Bush". And so it goes on, ending with "The Bush Today":

The Bush remains today with its reputation un-impaired... The Bush was acquired By Mr and Mrs D J Thomas in 1905. The late Mr Thomas was a much travelled man... He had been seven times round the world and had lived long in Hong Kong.

After his death his wife, Mrs Thomas, continued alone but despite running a busy pub she found the time and inclination to enjoy the thrills of early aviation:

On the 9th of July 1914 [she] made a flight from the Hendon Aerodrome, at a height of 2,500 feet around the neighbourhood in a Maurice Farman Biplane!

Into the twentieth century and Dylan's father apparently patronised his namesake's establishment, as a school colleague, J Morys Jones, who was a classics master at the Grammar School, remembers:

Of a Saturday you'd see him in tweeds, being the country gentleman. He'd sit in a corner of The Bush Hotel with his beer. They used to call him The Professor without being sure what he actually was.

Like father like son, and Dylan grew up to enjoy using The Bush as a place to meet friends, and

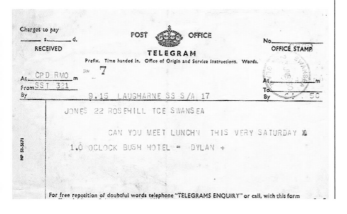

sometimes as a place to stay when he visited Swansea from London and West Wales, as this telegram sent from Laugharne to his pal Dr Daniel Jones indicates.

Apart from meeting Dan and others of the Kardomah Boys, Dylan would also meet in The Bush with another remarkable local character – the Rev Leon Atkin. Why remarkable? Well, herewith the start of a biographical article by D Ben Rees on Rev Atkin:

ATKIN, LEON (1902–1976), minister of the Social Gospel and a campaigner for the underclass in south Wales. Born in Spalding, Lincolnshire on 26 July 1902, the son of a gas manager, he was one of seven children. The family lived next door to the Methodist chapel and although they were Anglicans, Leon as a child attended their activities and he became a Methodist. The family moved in 1914 to Biddulph, and in 1916 he became a boy preacher, which brought him a great deal of publicity that he thoroughly enjoyed.

After serving an apprenticeship as an engineer he was accepted as a student for the ministry. Even at this time he had a series of confrontations with the college authorities but he was appointed Probationer Minister at St John's Church, Risca, Gwent, in 1930. He adopted the Social Gospel and challenged the militant Communists and the secularist movement in the mining valleys of Monmouthshire. Atkin held weekly open-air meetings in the tradition of his contemporary Donald Soper in London. For a whole year he debated every Friday night in a working men's club in Risca, with members of the Communist Party as well as with unbelievers who attended the Sunday evening services. As a rule 800 to 900 people would attend the service.

It goes on to paint a vivid picture of a man, who, after various clashes with the establishment, came to Swansea and ran St Paul's Church in his own eccentric fashion, developing his ministry among needy people. His care for the disadvantaged and the "down and outs" became known through his articles in the press, in particular through the *News of the World*. It is no wonder Dylan was proud to refer to Leon as "my padre". The two became regular drinking pals; Leon enjoyed a drink while taking his ministry into Swansea's pubs. Leon remembers a particular incident in the pub which strengthened their mutual respect for each other:

> there was a group of them used to go to The Bush sometimes: Dylan, Dan and the painter man (Fred Janes).

Leon describes how a local "businessman" who worked in the market, approached them in The Bush, because:

> he had an idea he could write poetry and he asked if "Dylan would read this, or let me read a line to him".

One of Dylan's group, unnamed but "half-drunk" and "being very crude", abused the would-be versifier, but Dylan stepped in and read the poem and gave the aspirant all the encouragement he could muster:

> Carry on working… Not bad… Carry on… Keep at it.

Leon was very moved by the incident and likened Dylan's response to the biblical text, "suffer little children" and he describes Dylan as a "Christian Socialist". In 1934 Dylan and Leon both attended the fascist rally held in Swansea when Sir Oswald Mosely took centre stage. They both attended in the spirit of opposition. Dylan went with his friend Bert Trick, "the communist grocer" from the Uplands. Dylan and Bert cowered in the wings observing events but Leon sat in the main hall and recounts his experience:

> [Mosely] began to speak. For an hour-and-a-half he spoke; from beginning to end, his speech consisted of a tirade against international Jewry. The Jews, he argued were responsible for everything bad on the planet… When he had finished he announced that he would take a few questions, but not oral questions. I could not resist writing on the back of my invite, my question, "I have been working for a Jew for quite a number of years. Ought I change my employer?"

Much to his surprise and delight Leon's question came out first, and Mosely answered in all seriousness:

> Certainly, I am sure if you looked round you would find a far more reliable one.

With that, Leon stood up in his full clerical attire, and with polite irony called out:

> Mr Mosely could you give me his name and address.

Realising he had been duped Mosely turned purple with rage and demanded, "Is this man a bona fide parson?" "Course he bloody is!" came the shouted retort and, as Leon puts it, "within a few seconds pandemonium reigned".

Leon Atkin was also a poet, and in 1947, a book of his work was published, *If Men Should Ask – Poems of War and Peace*. We don't know for sure if Dylan read this collection, which was made up of poems concerning his time as an army chaplain during the Second World War, but if he did he would have enjoyed the excerpts from Leon's prose poem/play *Uriah's Widow*, which contains Leon's thoughts on drink:

On Wine
To find the man – the undraped man within the man – give wine, good wine in plenty; until the sparkling cup o'erflow; until it put to sleep the watchful sentry of the servile soul… Then, with a neverfailing key, it will unlock the deepest dungeon of man's being and liberate a flock of tell-tale birds – some are vultures, some are doves; Deep in the mind of every man, deep buried by convention, there sits either a gibbering devil or a weeping angel:

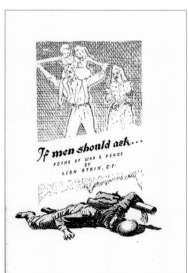

In wine, a man is what he would be. The drunkard seldom lies – except when sober! Give wine to the man who is ready to die – and you'll find him anon more ready to live! Music and wine were wedded in the scheme of God; they enlarge the heart; adding strange charm to all things – especially to weak things and to women; and wine will wash the shadows of the soul when bigotry has barred the door to beauty and to truth.

Surely, coming from a man of the cloth, even one as eccentric as Leon, Dylan would have seconded these emotions. But Atkin also wrote of Dylan:

he preferred beer. He did drink a lot, and I am prepared to admit he drank too much. In fact, I think he drank in proportion to the ugliness of the world in which he lived… he just used to hide behind a barrel, or try to drown his sorrows. He found they could swim, as they mostly do.

But although they often met and drank together Leon was to share one last poignant drink with Dylan. On a day in early October 1953, Dylan sent another telegram to Daniel Jones this time from Laugharne, demanding: "CAN YOU MEET BUSH 1.30 TODAY ON MY WAY TO AMERICA".

Dan describes, how this simple request became a very protracted session in his book *My Friend Dylan Thomas:*

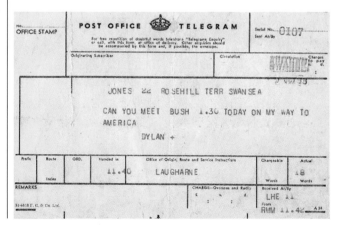

So began not one day, but nearly three full days full of enjoyment but heavy with guilt.

Daniel was guilty because he had "an almost impossible deadline" to meet and Dylan was guilty because he was overdue in London to leave for his fourth reading tour of America. As ever they banished these negative feelings and Dan describes how:

> on the morning of the last day… we went to several pubs, ending up at The Bush, where we drank till afternoon closing-time.

And then a mad rush to finally, and at last, get Dylan onto his train. Dan ran down the platform as Dylan:

> stood at the open window, waving one hand slightly with an exaggerated weakness and smiling an odd little smile… the last time I ever saw his face.

At some point in the proceedings Leon Atkin had joined Dylan in The Bush, a meeting that a local photographer, Tal L Jones, was to capture. His picture later made the local Swansea paper; the caption read, "Last photo of Dylan in Swansea".

Leon Atkin was to sum up Dylan thus:

> The only time I saw Dylan in a church was when his coffin was taken in for the funeral service… He lived, I suppose, more on faith than most parsons ever have tried to do. And no one could ever accuse him of daring to submit his talent to commercial interest. In fact, there were times when he looked like a tramp, and I suppose he didn't eat much more than a tramp. He always struck me as a man whose soul was so much

The Bush landlord, Rev Atkin and Dylan; his last drink in Swansea

> alive that he suffered. He suffered a lot, I think. But every action he seemed to make was, according to my unorthodox view, a religious action. It was an attempt to evaluate and appreciate and express beauty and something that was lovely… He was a perfectionist… poor old Dylan, he did just explode… you could almost say that he died in childbirth.

Dylan and Leon would have loved this headline, which appeared in a 1961 *South Wales Evening Post* supplement commemorating the twentieth anniversary of the Luftwaffe bombing of Swansea town centre. "Beer saved The Bush" screams the headline and readers are told how, on that dreadful night in 1941:

> As no water was available, more than fifty gallons of 'best draught' beer was used to put out fires.

Dylan and Leon would have wept fifty gallons of tears reading that last sentence!

BEER SAVED THE BUSH

BEER IS BEST, and it saved the Bush Hotel, Swansea, during the Blitz of 1941.

As no water was available, more than fifty gallons of the "best draught" beer was used to put out fires in six of the bedrooms.

The Hotel, which was established in the sixteenth century, has welcomed many distinguished guests, including Oliver Cromwell and Brian Curvis.

It has also seen many changes, but it was after the last World War that the most important changes took place.

The bedrooms referred to above were knocked down and the space used to construct a Steak Bar and Chicken Barbecue, where beer now plays its rightful role in washing down the best quality steaks at 6/6 and genuine barbecued chickens at 5/-.

The old kitchen has been converted into a Grill Room and the old Restaurant into a delightful Wine Lounge where one can have Sherry from the wood from the world's leading shippers for as little as 1/3 per large glass.

The Bush now proudly boasts of Six Bars, a Chicken Barbecue, a Grill Room, and a wonderful atmosphere all of its own.

The Manager and his wife, Mr. and Mrs. Pierre Pradere, are waiting to give you a warm and friendly welcome.

The Bush today

The Bush sadly went downhill in the 1980s. It had a brief resurgece at the start of the twenty-first century, getting a bright new coat of startling tangerine paint and a new name, *Creation and Eden*, and was proclaimed "Swansea's Premier Gay Destination". But that venture too proved unsustainable and the building today is now closed, somewhat dilapidated, and boarded up, but we are all eagerly awaiting its next incarnation.

Sadly, since I first wrote this, The Bush has been wilfully and wickedly demolished. Where the Luftwaffe failed, inept councils and planners have succeeded. This editorial from the local paper says it all:

Tuesday, July 16, 2013

NOW'S TIME TO STOP THE ROT

When it's gone, it's gone. Sadly, that is the fate of The Bush Hotel in Swansea's High Street. The pledge by Coastal Housing to retain some aspects of the building in its replacement is something at least.

But it's like going to Stonehenge to find the monument has been knocked down and they've retained one of the original stones at the entrance to the supermarket which has replaced it. The heart and soul of the building has gone – all that is left is an echo.

Mumbles

The two Mumbles "mammaries"

Oh, woe, woe, woe unto Mumbles and the oystered beer.
– *Dylan Thomas, letter to Trevor Hughes, 1934*

… a rather nice village, despite its name.
– *Dylan Thomas to Pamela Hansford Johnson, 1934*

WRITING to Pamela Hansford Johnson in 1931, Dylan offers her a description of one of his average Swansea days which draws to a close thus:

After tea I read or write again, as haphazardly as before, until six o'clock. I then go to Mumbles (remember the Women of Mumbles Head) a rather nice village despite its name, right on the edge of the sea. First I call at The Marine, then The Antelope and then The Mermaid. If there is no rehearsal, I continue to commune with these two legendary creatures.

In 1936 Dylan was offering poems to an editor friend, Desmond Hawkins, who was behind a literary magazine called *Purpose*. Dylan was ambivalent about titles, but he suggested that his poem beginning "Today this insect, and the world I breathe" which Hawkins was to publish, might also be titled "Necrophilia in Mumbles". Mumbles was apparently named for the two breast-shaped (mammary) islands at the end of the bay, or less prosaically, for the sounds made by of the sea rolling over the stony beaches.

In 1949 Dylan presented a radio broadcast called *Swansea and the Arts*. In the programme some of Dylan's closest Swansea friends spoke of what the town meant to them and the poet Vernon Watkins ended his tribute thus:

A town speaks through its art. Most towns speak with an impediment, and there are some towns that can't speak at all, but only snore and rattle, and make hideous mechanical noises. I like Swansea because Swansea has a natural impediment: it speaks with the Mumbles.

In recent years Mumbles became very popular with students and young folk on stag and hen parties,

The Mumbles Train

The Swansea and Mumbles Railway was the world's first passenger railway service.

Originally built under an Act of Parliament of 1804 to move limestone from the quarries of Mumbles to Swansea and to the markets beyond, it carried the world's first fare-paying railway passengers on March 25th, 1807 (the same day the British Parliament abolished the transportation of slaves from Africa). It later moved from horse power to steam locomotion, and finally converted to electric trams, before closing in January 1960.

Dylan recalls this local wonder in his radio script *Holiday Memory* where he writes fondly of, "the trams that hissed like ganders took us all to the beautiful beach". In 1935 he writes a letter from Ireland, to Bert Trick, steeped in "hiraeth". He dreams of:

who would challenge themselves to complete The Mumbles Mile, which involved having a pint (or short) in every one of the nine main pubs that nestled along the seafront. It was often a messy business and as the pubs have closed, so has its popularity, and nowadays Mumbles has a more upmarket range of smart bars and restaurants.

Oystermouth Train

walking past your shop to the trainstop, and rattling along to a beery and fleshy Oystermouth.

Dylan never witnessed the demise of the Mumbles Train and like many other locals he would surely have disapproved of the decision to scrap it. The train, and its destination, stayed with him throughout his life, and it gets a mention in his last great masterpiece, *Under Milk Wood*, where the character of the fourth drowned sailor introduces himself as:

> Alfred Pomeroy Jones, sea lawyer, born in Mumbles, sung like a linnet, crowned you with a flagon, tattooed with mermaids, thirst like a dredger, died of blisters.

Swansea & Oystermouth Railway

The Mermaid

Oystermouth Road, Mumbles

LIKE EVERY SWANSEA CHILD Dylan Thomas would have been taken on occasional outings on the train around the bay to Mumbles. In his teens, when he joined the Swansea Little Theatre, whose rehearsals rooms were in the village, he became a regular independent visitor to the village. Dylan had begun to act as a very young lad. In her fine book on Dylan and Vernon *Portrait of a Friend* (1983), Gwen Watkins described an early episode when Dylan performed in a play when he was a pupil at Mrs Hole's kindergarten in Mirador Crescent, Uplands:

> Dylan played to the gallery, instead of playing the sedate colonel he was cast as, he blew orange peel through the newspaper he was supposed to be reading and rushed about the stage, beating the air with his stick until the curtain came down.

A fine beginning to an acting career that saw him go on to take the part of Edward Stanton in John Drinkwater's *Abraham Lincoln* in the Swansea Grammar School production and, as a 15-year old, he took a lead role in the school production of

Drinkwater's *Oliver Cromwell*. Dylan's performance in the title role gained good notices in the local press:

> Oliver Cromwell, in spite of the fact that physically he was not up to the part... Still he bore himself with poise and dignity, his enunciation was good, and he succeeded in conveying the impression of courage, strength and resolution in a part that made heavy demands upon the actor.

After a spell with the local YMCA Junior Players, Dylan joined his older sister Nancy at the prestigious Swansea Little Theatre and they rehearsed and sometimes performed in a church hall above the seafront, at Southend, Mumbles. He had by now left school and left his first job on the local paper, but with time on his hands and, inspired by his school friend Wynford Vaughan Thomas, Dylan joined the group and he began to enjoy regular trips on the Mumbles Train for rehearsals and performances.

Dylan rehearsing with the Swansea Little Theatre Players

Undoubtedly acting was one of his deepest interests, but on route for rehearsals he was apt to pay frequent visits to the many fine pubs of Mumbles. He was soon writing to a friend of the joys of The Mermaid and The Antelope which he referred to as "these two legendary creatures". Dylan, aged 18, wrote to his friend Trevor Hughes about the temptations of the Mumbles pubs which were already luring him away from writing poetry:

> I am playing in Noel Coward's Hay Fever at the little theatre this season. Much of my time is taken up with rehearsals. Much of my time is taken up with concerts, deaths, meetings and dinners. It's odd, but between all these I manage to become drunk at least four nights a week. Muse or Mermaid?

Dylan's good friend and co-reporter on the *Post*, Charlie Fisher, recalls:

> He asked me, I think in The Mermaid Tavern in the Mumbles, "Charles do you like beer?" I said, "Not really." "I do," he said. "I like the taste of it."

Another friend, Wynford Vaughan Thomas, himself a fine broadcaster and legendary bon viveur, recounts a Mumbles incident as a member of the theatre in his autobiography *Trust to Talk* (1980):

> I never played any outstanding role but, to my surprise, was once invited to perform as Lorenzo in The Merchant of Venice. Dylan, to his equal surprise, was cast as Stephano, servant to Portia. Now Stephano hasn't a great deal to do, and Dylan found that he had plenty of chances to slip down

to the nearby pub of Fulton's Vaults, where he happily refreshed himself at regular intervals. My big moment came in Act Five, when I arrived with Jessica at Portia's garden at night and together we declaimed that magical verbal duet which begins, "The moon shines bright. In such a night as this…" I turned to give Dylan his cue, "Who comes so fast in silence of the night?"

The answer was no one! Dylan was still wrapped in the silence of Fulton's Vaults. I had no option but to soldier on and invite Jessica to have a restful sit-down while I launched myself into the famous description of the heavens echoing to the music of the spheres. Still, I had to get back to the plot and surely Dylan must have returned by now! Boldly I cried again, "I hear a sound. Here comes the messenger!" Shakespeare never wrote such words but I was desperate. Again no sound off stage. I looked around wildly and then gasped out to Jessica: "Did'st thou hear not what I said about the heavens? Then sit once more, fair Jessica. Pay more attention." On I went through the speech again… This time, I vowed, Dylan would hear… I fairly bellowed, "Come on, come on, thou sluggish messenger."

There was a slight shuffle backstage. I hissed through my teeth, "Who comes – at last – in silence of the night?" On came a wobbling and distinctly happy Dylan who slapped me on the back and announced to the astonished audience, "It's me, old boy. Don't you recognise me? Sorry I'm late. What do I say next?"

The Little Theatre players favoured The Mermaid. Andrew Lycett, in his biography *Dylan Thomas, A New Life* (2003), describes how the "the thespian banter flowed with drinks" and he goes on to describe another incident involving Dylan and Wynford:

Once, after a widely reported rabies epidemic, Dylan and friend Wynford Vaughan-Thomas… used this as some spontaneous horseplay. They went down on all fours and crawled around the floor of the pub, pretending to be rabid dogs, biting people's ankles. When Dylan tried this on the actress Ruby Graham, she feigned anger and shooed him out of the door. She was astonished to see him continue across the pavement to a lamp-post. "I thought he was going to pee on it," she recalled. Instead, he bit on it, leaving him with a broken tooth for the rest of his life. (Afterwards, he used to tell her he remembered her every time he smiled.)

Dylan refers to this incident in his radio play *Return Journey*, when he writes this wonderful, irreverent self-description:

and above medium height. Above medium height for Wales, I mean, he's five foot six-and-a-half. Thick blubber lips; snub nose; curly mousebrown hair; one front tooth broken after playing a game called Cats and Dogs in The Mermaid, Mumbles.

Eileen Davies, who appeared with Dylan in *Beaux Stratagem*, recalls meeting him off the train at Oystermouth station. His first words to her were a grumbling:

Oh dear we've got to go in and under-act again.

Instead they end up in The Mermaid, where Dylan urged them all to join in an impromptu word game:

Take any noun describing something on the table. Then let's find an adjective that is the most opposite. For example, see that jelly. There you are; "static jelly".

It seemed a surrealist frame of mind came early to Dylan Thomas. The Mermaid also features in a little-known play that Dylan wrote into a letter sent in 1934 to Pamela Hansford Johnson. It is called *Spajma and Salnady; or Who Shot the Emu? A One Act Play Never to be Presented.* Dan Jones, commenting on how Dylan as a teenager was much more sophisticated than himself, describes how on:

> almost every Sunday afternoon, when the pubs were closed, he played gin rummy for small stakes at The Mermaid.

It would seem that one of these afternoons inspired this curious play. The names of the hero and heroine are anagrams of the poet and his correspondent. In one section of the play Dylan writes:

(For the first time Spajma perceives her companion is walking... with a hobble and a stick)

SPAJMA: *(with interest)* Why are you limping?

SALNADY: I have sprained my ankle, and very painful it is, too. It happened like this: *(Spajma looks very bored, but he continues)* On Sunday nights it is my custom to go to my Mermaid Hotel – you can't have an official drink in Wales on a Sunday, of course – creep up the stairs and into the manageress's room where, in the company of the manageress herself – a stout, charming, middle-aged girl with red hair and a thirst – a dim barmaid, my dress designing toper, I consume too much out of too many bottles, argue on obscure religious points and listen to the gramophone. Last Sunday I stayed longer than usual, and, in attempting to go downstairs to the bar, slipped and fell a considerable way. My ankle went up like a balloon and I retired to bed, the manageress's bandages, sympathetic stories from the toper, and more beer. There was slight annoyance when I arrived home in time for dinner next day. The untidiness of my speech is due to the fact I am still in great pain.

SPAJMA: There's a pity, you sot. But you are all too young for this lordishness, aren't you? You probably think it's very smart and wicked of you. It's just childish.

SALNADY: Possibly. But it must be drink or drug, you know.

One can only comment along the lines of – many a true word is spoken in jest. Dylan's relationship with Pamela was shortly to end, but before it did she made a visit to Swansea (with her mother in tow as chaperone) to visit Dylan and his family, and it was in The Mermaid Hotel that Pamela and her mother stayed. Dylan would later stay there himself when he and Caitlin came back to Swansea and his parents were moving house.

Dylan continued to visit The Mermaid whenever he visited Mumbles. In the spring of 1934 he writes to Trevor Hughes describing a depressing visit there with Daniel Jones:

> Last night, Dan and I, none too bright, for the womb of The Mermaid was empty, and the radiogram blaring, discovered we had too little feeling... I don't know why or what, but last night we who had no feelings spoke passionately... as we swilled and wallowed, damning the conventions as we took the bus home and lied when we got there.

The cheque stub illustrated shows that Dylan was back with Dan in The Mermaid as late as 1951 when, the evidence of Dan's cheque stub would suggest they had a much better time. A bar bill of £4 in those

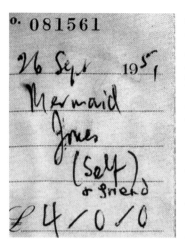

days represents quite a bibulous time and on the stub Dylan, at pains to take some of the blame (or credit), has added "& friend" under Dan's "Self".

Another of Dylan's friends from school was Bob Rees, a good all-round sportsman who acted as a kind of minder to young Thomas. Bob went on to become a history teacher in London, but in his youth he too enjoyed the dubious pleasures of The Mermaid with Dylan. In 1935 Bob asked Dylan to sign his copy of Dylan's first book, *18 Poems*, and Dylan obliged with more than just a signature. He inscribed the book:

To Bob – One of the Reo's The Mermaid knocked about a bit.

Some twenty years ago, in my antiquarian bookseller guise, I bought this book from Bob and he explained the significance of the inscription thus:

The reference, as I found out, was to a music hall song of Marie Lloyd's *I'm one of the ruins that Cromwell knocked about a bit*. I also found out that T S Eliot wrote movingly about Marie Lloyd and especially, about this song. "The Reos" were Dylan and me. Reo was the name of a wine, inferior, but cheap. The Mermaid was the hotel on the seafront at Southend, on the Mumbles Road.

I had called on Dylan to find him propped up, sitting with a clipboard on his knees, writing and correcting. We went out, first to several hotels near the docks, then by train, to The Mermaid. Beer was always the preferred drink, but, money running short, we had to come to a decision. Something had to be kept for the train fare back. With the little which was left and the kindly help of a friendly barmaid, we bought a large bottle of Reo wine, which she found in some odd corner of the cellar. We left the returning train at the slip and walked up towards the Uplands in cheerful mood, extolling the virtues of Reo. It was wintertime. The pavements had icy patches. Our progress with occasional slips was not always steady. On our return we were, thus, "knocked about a bit". Still cheerful we reached Dylan's house. An irate Mrs Thomas suddenly appeared and I fled.

Even Vernon Watkins, Dylan's usually sober and restrained friend, succumbed to The Mermaid's tempting charms on at least one occasion. Gwen Watkins describes the incident, and the poem by Vernon that it inspired, in the chapter entitled "Drink" in her book *Portrait of a Friend*:

On October 27, 1936, Vernon spent the evening of Dylan's birthday with him. They started off with a drink at The Bay View Hotel, then took turns to ride Vernon's bicycle along the Mumbles Road to Oystermouth, ending up at Dylan's favourite pub, The Mermaid. Vernon recorded this occasion in a long poem called 'Sailors on the Moving Land', which was published in *Life and Letters Today* in 1949 – although the first of its many drafts is on pre-war paper, and the last is dated 1956, three years after Dylan's death.

The occasion was a comic one, yet the poem is serious. In drunkenness, inhibitions disappear, and perhaps confidences were made which would not have been made sober; at any rate, Vernon perceived something of the essential tragedy of Dylan's life and personality.

Before the safety curtain dropped
Upon all knowledge, while we stopped
The edge of distance, by degrees
October brought no flying grains
Rustling behind the Mumbles trains
Passing our faces where time stopped:
Leaving this music of the tunnelled seas.

Dylan and Vernon were already tipsy as they threaded their uncertain way along the narrow Oystermouth pavements, past the shops, still, in those pre-war days, open till nine or ten o'clock. They moved erratically towards The Mermaid:

"I have a bicycle that is not mine."

"The round moon racing through the clouds is fine."

"I have seen Lamprey's marble crossed by eels."

"Must we be mastered by the moving wheels?'

So to the inner smoke:
the quarrelling air:
Angry jolting of a chair:
Edge of the darkness' knife:
confessions of despair;
The bitter mermaid sang her worst.
Neither throat could slake its thirst.

When the pub closed, they were turned out into the street, that heaved like the sea under their feet, and started up hill past Oystermouth Castle, sometimes taking turns to push, or lean over the bicycle, and sometimes discovering that neither of them was pushing it, so that they had to retrace their steps to find it lying in the gutter. Once, in the bright moonlight, the shadow of Vernon's head appeared to have grown horns (in reality the shadow of the handlebars). Dylan became terrified, insisting that he was walking with the devil, and it was with great difficulty that he was persuaded to go on.

So from Oystermouth's nets of Wales
Followed by the fishes' tails
And every print and spoor of grief:
Where the dull trees were lopped of every leaf
We climbed through darkness where you danced about:
Gay as a babbling thief.
Oystermouth Castle floated round
Two with a bicycle, two men with horns.
Two shadowed quarrellers pushing two moons.

It took Vernon three hours to cover the seven miles to Pennard. He could never remember where Dylan left him. What he did remember was that he had seen for the first time the profound unhappiness that lived beneath the mask. Gwen concludes:

It was excuse enough in Vernon's mind for any subsequent drunkenness on Dylan's part; if he drank too much it was because his suffering was too great to be borne. Usually, however, Vernon discounted stories of Dylan's drunkenness as exaggerations; this was the only time he had seen Dylan drunk, and it was, after all, his birthday celebration.

Perhaps we should let Dylan have the last word on this, one of his favourite pubs. Writing from Ireland in 1935 to his friend Bert Trick in Swansea, he declares:

But this is by no means a despondent letter. Words are coming nicely, and the rain can't get through the roof. I have a blazing turf fire and the only sound is the sea's on the million stones. I have a beard, too, a curly ginger growth, neatly irregular, sweetly disorderly. I'll keep it for good, I think, or long enough for the Tricks and Thomases & My Mumbles Mermaid (bless her hair and her tail) to admire and finger it.

The bitter mermaid sang her worst. Neither throat could slakk her thirst.

Vernon Watkins.

The Mermaid today

Alas today The Mermaid Hotel is no more. It closed and fell empty a couple of decades ago, and then it suffered two quite dreadful fires. The grand old building was no longer safe and was demolished. A new luxury apartment block was built in its place. However the ground floor is still open to visitors as a popular restaurant and bar that has kept the original name – *The Mermaid of Mumbles*, and the façade is decorated with sculptures of very buxom mermaids.

The Antelope

Oystermouth Road, Mumbles

THE ANTELOPE is the second "legendary creature" to be found in Dylan's mythical Mumbles pub zoo. The pub is situated on the corner of Mumbles Road and Village Lane and the pub sign shows that the antelope in question was clearly not a wild beast but a sailing ship. The pub was originally called The Oystermouth Castle Hotel but in the late 1860s the pub was taken over by David Rees who had kept a pub in Swansea town called The Antelope and he chose to bring this name with him.

In its early years the pub earned a reputation for being a pretty rough dive. In 1888, the then landlord, Henry James, was summonsed for opening on a Sunday, and supplying a pint(!!!) of rum to a seaman, Edmund Bevan. That was crime enough, but made much worse when Bevan, having enjoyed his pint, assaulted a local police sergeant. Could it be that this scoundrel was the precursor of *Under Milk Wood*'s Curly Bevan, who from his watery grave confesses to Captain Cat:

Tell my auntie it was me that pawned the ormolu clock.

And then woefully asks:

And who brings coconuts and shawls and parrots to my Gwen now?

The Antelope was still a rough house going into the twentieth century. In 1907 it only just about kept its licence in the face of accusations of disorderly and riotous conduct. It was described as a "poor house of poor construction" but it managed to stay open. It was another pub situated just too conveniently close to the Swansea Little Theatre rehearsal hall; too tempting for Dylan to nip in for a quick refreshment between scenes.

It may well have been one of the pubs that contributed to Dylan's rift with the Little Theatre. By 1934 Dylan had risen in the company's pecking order and he was being offered major roles. Thus it was that in early 1934 he was cast as the male lead in the translated French play *Martine*. However this was to be his first encounter with the director Miss Doreen Goodridge! She ran her own drama school in Brynmill and was used to having 100 per cent commitment and dedication from her pupils. It would appear that there was a clash of character between the director and her leading man – the unbending disciplinarian versus the free spirit. But preparations went well, right up until the dress rehearsal the night before the play was to open. The programme was printed, with Dylan heading the cast. But it was not to be.

Ethel Ross, a stalwart of the Little Theatre (and the sister-in-law of Dylan's pal Fred Janes), wrote an interesting pamphlet on *Dylan Thomas and the Amateur*

Theatre and describes events at the dress rehearsal:

It was customary for the young men of the theatre and the more daring girls, when not wanted on stage, to nip out… Naturally players were often called in vain and someone would be sent post-haste to fetch them from the bar. Some producers put up with it better than others, but Doreen Goodridge, irritated to extremity, warned Thomas, who thought he had time for "a quick one", that if he left he needn't come back. He went.

Despite the consequences, the unbending Miss Goodridge kept to her threat and turned to another stalwart of the company, Malcolm Graham, to take over the role. He had first to read the part but swiftly committed it to memory and the show went on. The local press reported the debacle, describing Miss Goodridge as suffering "as hard a parcel of luck as any producer can have; her chief male character failed her within 24 hours". Malcolm Graham is praised for "doing the pluckiest thing" but even he could not prevent the atmosphere on the opening night being "a little overladen".

But perhaps it was the right time for Dylan to move on. Already a poem or two of his had appeared in London periodicals, and his appearances in the Poet's Corner section of the *Sunday Referee* had led to a dense correspondence with a fellow contributor, Pamela Hansford Johnson. Just a week or so after he was supposed to "star" in *Martine*, Dylan left for London for his first meeting with Pamela, which led to her becoming his first serious girlfriend. Even more importantly before the year was out his first book, *18 Poems*, was published and his literary career had begun to take off.

He did make a couple of appearances in Little Theatre revivals – reprising his roles in Noel Coward's *Hay Fever* and Ackland's *Strange Orchestra* and later he would do occasional

Miss Doreen Goodridge.

School of Dramatic Art

55, BRYN ROAD, SWANSEA.

Principal - Doreen Goodridge

*Diplomeé Royal Academy
of Dramatic Art, London*
Gold Medallist, A.L.A.M. (Elocution)

Individual and Class Tuition.   Professional Coaching given to Dramatic Societies

Speech Training, Stage Deportment and Technique, Make-up, etc.
Shakespeare.   Old Comedy.   Modern Drama.

AT THE LITTLE THEATRE.

Poet's Fancy on the Stage

"MARTINE," A PLAY OF DELICATE CHARM

"MARTINE," a translation from the French which Miss Doreen Goodridge produced at the Swansea Little Theatre last night, is a delicate trifle that calls for almost as much from its audience as its players. It deals with those elusive situations in life that are as eloquently described in the pauses between conversations as in the dialogue itself. It is a poet's fancy, real romanticism trembling always upon the verges of true comedy. It calls for sympathy and understanding.

Miss Goodridge last night had as hard a parcel of luck as any producer can have: her chief male character failed her, and within 24 hours Mr. Malcolm Graham, doing the pluckiest thing associated with his relations with the Little Theatre, was wrestling with it on the stage. It was indeed an excellent act, for which he will gratefully be remembered; and to-night he will be more within the skin of the part; but last night it would be idle to deny that the atmosphere was a little overladen for a play of such subtle charm.

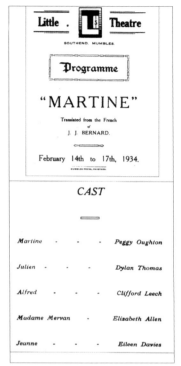

acting work for the BBC – but from this point onwards it was a literary rather than a theatrical life that he pursued. Later when he returned to Swansea and Mumbles, he would still call into The Antelope and would be seen sitting quietly in front of the fire scribbling on scraps of paper, but sadly at the end of the night the landlady would gather any discarded scraps and throw them on the flames!

The name that stands out when thinking about Dylan and The Antelope is that of Timothy Perkins. Tim was yet another remarkable Swansea character and also a well-respected member of the Swansea Little Theatre. He described his encounters with Dylan in a TV programme about *Great Welsh Cafés*. The series started with a look at a day in the life of Swansea's famous Kardomah Café, frequented by Dylan Thomas and his friends, The Kardomah Boys, in the 1930s. Dylan described it as "The Kardomah – My Home Sweet Homah". In the programme Tim, by then aged 89 and still looking upright and

distinguished, recalled seeing Dylan in the Kardomah every Saturday morning with his friends: the composer Daniel Jones, artist Fred Janes, broadcaster Wynford Vaughan Thomas and poet Vernon Watkins. But he admits that:

> [Dylan] wasn't really my cup of tea. I thought him a bit of a show-off. We would say hello and then he would go and sit at one table, and I would go and sit at another.

Despite his reservations, Tim went on to be one of the founder members of the Dylan Thomas Society of Great Britain and its first chairman. Tim declared, "No-one would be more astonished than Dylan himself to learn that I had started all this adulation!" The inaugural meeting of the society was held in Swansea on November 9th 1977 and was attended

A Dylan Thomas Society poetry reading in The Antelope – Tim, splendidly coifed as ever, is on the right

by Dylan's daughter, Aeronwy Thomas Ellis, who with her husband Trefor, presented a programme of readings from her father's work.

Before all this, in 1950, Tim took over from his parents as licensee and landlord of The Antelope. He brought to the place his own suave and sophisticated style, which saw the pub transformed from its disreputable past and become a smart and popular place for a new upmarket clientele. Tim's particular penchant was for Pimms, served with "half of Swansea Market's fruit stalls in the glass!"

Tim died in 1999 but his fame as a fine host became legendary and he began to attract a celebrity crowd, with the likes of actors Emlyn Williams, Anthony Hopkins, Wilfred Bramble, Tom Bell and Kenneth Williams joining sportsmen, such as Garfield Sobers, and local heroes like Ryan Davies, Kingsley Amis and Michael Heseltine. They all enjoyed the particular urbane and classy atmosphere that Tim generated. Apparently Dylan visited, both back in the dingy 30s and in the smart 50s, but he has not gone on record as to which incarnation he preferred!

The Antelope today

As we go to print this legendary pub is temporarily closed waiting for yet another makeover.

Gower

DYLAN THOMAS always saw himself as an urban creature; a lover of the town and the city; of interiors rather than open spaces; of busy roads rather than country lanes. He wrote to Vernon Watkins from Cornwall in 1936:

> Here the out-of-doors is very beautiful but it's a strange country to me… and I'd rather the bound slope of a suburban hill… I am not a countryman; I stand for the provincial drive, the morning café, the evening pub.

However in his youth he enjoyed, and would sing the praises of the Gower Peninsula. Writing to Pamela Hansford Johnson in 1933, he describes Gower as:

> a very beautiful peninsula, some miles from the blowsy town and so far the tea-shop philistines have not spoilt the more beautiful of its bays… Gower as a matter of fact is one of the loveliest sea-coast stretches in the whole of Britain and some of its villages are as obscure, as little inhabited and as lovely as they were a hundred years ago.

(at this point in the letter Dylan inserted a note in the margin which says – "*THIS SOUNDS LIKE A PASSAGE FROM A TOURIST GUIDE*"). In an effort to make himself sound romantic and interesting, he describes to Pamela how he loves:

GOWER

VOLUME SIX

The Gower Society Journal – Dylan Thomas Memorial Issue

up to three church services on his weekend visits but it was here that he imbibed his deep knowledge of the Bible that infuses his work, and where his uncle's preaching style, laced with hell-fire and brimstone and steeped in Welsh "hwyl" entered his psyche and would later colour his own distinctive booming style of delivering poetry and prose on the radio and in public performances.

The critic James A Davies writes in his book *Dylan Thomas's Places* (1987):

> Gower for Thomas was a crucial place… youthful memories of Gower provide material for his Portrait stories… and the scenery, in particular the seascapes, cliffs and wild-life, was an important general influence on his poetry.

walking alone over the very desolate Gower cliffs, communing with the cold and quietness.

Later Dylan would often visit his friend Vernon Watkins who lived on the cliffs at Pennard. Vernon would drag a reluctant Dylan along for cliff walks and beach rambles but he could not get Dylan to join him in his regular swims in the clear waters of Hunt's Cove. As a young boy, Dylan was often taken to the Gower village of Newton, which is above Mumbles, to visit his Aunt Dosie, his mother's sister. She had married the Rev David Rees, minister at Paraclete Congregational Church, and the couple lived in the adjoining Manse (which is where I now live!). Dylan was not too happy about having to attend

Young Dylan's weekend retreat to his Aunt Dosie's in Newton

The Worm's Head Hotel

Rhossili

THE BAR of this hotel, set at the western-most tip of Gower, must surely boast one of the most beautiful and scenic views of any bar in the world. Rhossili Down is the highest point on Gower, and it offers views of the peninsula as well as views across the sea to West Wales, Lundy Island and the north Devon coast. It also boasts an example of curious synchronicity that I love: as you gaze down onto the immense beach at low tide the jagged timbers of a skeletal old wreck reach up out of the sand – it is the wreck of a vessel *The Helvetia*. Dylan must have gazed down at it not knowing that 30 years later he would lose his precious manuscript of *Under Milk Wood* by leaving it in a London pub – named *The Helvetia*!

The hotel is perched on the clifftop at the edge of the village and it is a good place to stop for a drink before walking out to Worm's Head, the rugged tip of the land that Dylan describes as "the very promontory of depression". Local lore asserts that the name is a derivative of the Norse Viking "vorm" which is their word for a sea serpent, and the Old English "vurm" for "dragon" – and that is just what this elongated craggy island looks like from out at sea. The Worm gets cut off by the sea, but at low tide a causeway allows walkers to visit the island for a few hours and often visitors can get stranded. In his youth Dylan loved to walk on Gower – or at least that is what he told Pamela Hansford Johnson. In his early letters to her, he describes Rhossili bay as the "wildest, bleakest and barrenest I know" and tells her it is his favourite destination on his "medicinal walks".

It is a walk to Rhossili that provides the backdrop to Dylan's melancholy and poignant short story "Who Do You Wish Was With Us", first published in *Portrait of the Artist as a Young Dog*. The story is a fictionalised account of a hike to Rhossili that Dylan took with his pal Trevor Hughes, who Dylan calls Ray Price in the story. Trevor Hughes moved to London before Dylan, and in a letter to him sent from Swansea in 1933, Dylan urges him to:

> Remember the Worm, read a meaning into its symbol – a serpents head rising out of the clean sea.

In the story the two lads start out from the Uplands intending to walk some twenty miles to Rhossili and out onto the Worm. But the boys tire of walking after covering half the distance and jump on a bus. Once there, they cross the causeway and get to the very end of the Worm. Dylan is ecstatic and declares from the top of the "humped and serpentine body":

Instead of becoming small on the great rock poised between sky and sea, I felt myself the size of a breathing building... as I said, "Why don't we live here always? Always and always. Build a bloody house and live like bloody kings!"

But sadly Dylan's pal cannot join in with this joyful fantasy as Ray is constantly haunted with memories of his dead epileptic father:

I used to hold my father down on the bed when he had fits... Father thought I was trying to murder him on the bed.

These memories are exacerbated by the more recent loss of his brother to the scourge of tuberculosis:

I had to change the sheets twice a day for my brother, there was blood on everything.

Dylan tries to lift the mood by fooling about on the rocks and cliffs and Ray tries to join in but when Dylan, totally overcome with excitement, keeps asking and asking him:

Who do you wish was with us?... Who would you like to be here on the rock with us?... Who do you wish was with us Ray?

The despondent Ray can only reply:

I wish my brother was with us, I wish Harry was here. I wish he was here now, at this moment, on this rock.

Trevor Hughes would later give an account of the actual incident to the Canadian-based broadcaster Colin Edwards (the complete archive of interviews is now in the National Library in Aberystwyth). In his interview Hughes describes the day:

at the end of September 1931, I was to move to London... on the Saturday morning Dylan asked if I would spend the day down the Gower Peninsula. So we got down to Rhossili – that was a glorious day. We walked out to Worm's Head... I sat on the edge of the cliffs... Dylan had some paper and a pencil with him and he would say, "Well now, give me the last word in each line, and I will write the poem."

He describes how they got cut off and were marooned until one o'clock in the morning before the coastguards came and rescued them. But they still had to get back to Swansea and had to walk almost all of the thirty miles:

Dylan got very, very tired... he was very young, only seventeen, a few times he sat down in the middle of the road and declared he wasn't going another inch.

Another story in the same collection, "Extraordinary Little Cough", is also set at Rhossili and is again firmly rooted in Dylan's real life schoolboy adventures. It is the story of a bunch of boys in their early teens, going off for a fortnight's camping holiday in this magical place.

The story centres on a cruel dare that two local bully boys – Brazell and Skully – make to Little Cough who is challenged to run the length of the beach –some three or four miles. He succeeds but misses all the fun with local girls and music. It would appear that much of this story is based on fact; a school friend of Dylan's, John Bennett, enjoyed just such a camping holiday with Dylan at Rhossili and has confirmed that they enjoyed the exact music Dylan describes – "No No Nanette" – and there were three girls camping there.

And the bully boy Brazell; he was also a real acquaintance, immortalised in a piece in Swansea Grammar School magazine, where it is reported:

> We hear great things of Brazel (sic) and his goal kicking!

And Dylan's love of the tip of this rugged peninsula extended late into adulthood. In 1940 when Dylan and Caitlin had to leave Laugharne because of mounting debts, they had no alternative but to move in with Dylan's parents in the rather small house they had retired to in Bishopston, a Swansea west suburb. It was a difficult time for them, and Caitlin in

particular, was very unhappy. The only person pleased by the situation was Vernon Watkins who had his great friend nearby, and they could meet regularly and discuss their poems. In an effort to cheer them up Vernon arranged for his friend Wyn Lewis to drive them all to Rhossili for a bracing walk out onto the Worm. But it almost ended very badly when they very nearly got themselves stranded. Let Gwen Watkins take up the story:

> Dylan and Vernon were walking some way behind Wyn and Caitlin when they first became aware that the pools between the Worm and the mainland were filling up. Wyn and Caitlin began to run and jump to dry land, but Dylan, podgy and soon beginning to pant, became almost frantic at the prospect of spending eight hours on the Worm while Caitlin was alone on the beach with the ravishingly handsome Wyn. Knee-deep in waves and completely breathless, he was finally dragged by Vernon up the sand.

Wyn had his camera with him and they all took turns to snap a series of group photos recording the afternoon and as Gwen comments, "Dylan still looks serious, almost sullen, at his escape from jealousy".

In 1948 he writes to Vernon Watkins from Oxford, after just having read "Extraordinary Cough" on the radio:

> I wish you had heard my story about Rhossili. I wish I were in Rhossili.

And he did almost go and live there. In 1953 Dylan was back in Swansea to record some radio programmes, he once more returned to Rhossili, this

Caitlin's snap of Dylan, Wyn Lewis and Vernon at Rhossili

time with Caitlin and his friends Dan and Irene Jones, to visit his old schoolmate Guido Heller, who had taken on the running of the hotel, which at that time was still unlicensed. Looking out at the spectacular view, Guido pointed out to Dylan the Old Rectory, a lone deserted house set in splendid isolation on the downs which roll out towards the vast expanse of sandy beach. Dylan was again becoming bored by Laugharne, and once again under pressure to settle his debts. The wild isolated eighteenth-century Old Rectory, or The Parsonage as it is known locally, seemed the ideal safe haven, as Guido remembers:

> he suddenly as an afterthought, turned to me and said, "Tell me, where's the nearest pub?" So I said it's either at Llangennith or down at The Ship in Port Eynon. "God," he said, "I could never stick that, that's too far away."

The idea was swiftly abandoned – and had he moved there he might have escaped his creditors but would instead have had to deal with the spirits and demons that local legend has haunting the place! Dylan would later describe it in a letter to the poet Idris Davies as:

> an old & ratty rectory owned by a batty farmer.

Splendid though it was, and is, Dylan would never get to live in Rhossili.

The Worm's Head Hotel today

Today the hotel is a thriving bar and hotel with a reputation for good hearty food and occasional music nights. And the Old Rectory is still there, and is available to rent from the National Trust, but be warned, it is their most popular property and is always booked well in advance. However this did not prevent the Wales Tourist Board choosing, for some bizarre reason, to airbrush it out of their 2002 promotional pictures, as this newspaper article highlights!

FAMOUS: The Old Rectory where Welsh poet Dylan Thomas used to stay with his family

VANISHED: The tourist board decided the Gower Coast looked better without it

Carmarthenshire

THE OLD COUNTY of Carmarthenshire was an important and nostalgic place for Dylan Thomas. His father was born in Johnstown, just outside Carmarthen town and his mother's family were from rural farming stock and lived in small villages such as Llangain and Llanybri. Throughout his life Dylan had visited and stayed with many of his relations and many are still living the area.

It was at the Infirmary just outside Carmarthen that Dylan's aunt, Ann Jones, died in 1933. She was the subject of one of Dylan's greatest poems "After the Funeral", and her farm was the farm celebrated in Dylan's greatest poem *Fern Hill*:

> *And as I was green and carefree, famous among the barns*
> *About the happy yard and singing as the farm was home:*
> *In the sun that is young once only.*

Fern Hill farm was where, as a boy, Dylan spent his many holidays. This was the farm where the biblical stories he got from Paraclete Chapel Sunday School were reinforced by the strength of Welsh nonconformity, but this is also Merlin's country and these Bible stories became melded in Dylan's imagination with the Celtic Mabinogion tales. It

CASEG BROADSHEET No 5.

From
IN MEMORY
OF ANN JONES

AFTER the feast of tear-stuffed time and thistles
In a room with a stuffed fox and a stale fern,
I stand, for this memorial's sake, alone
In the snivelling hours with dead, humped Ann
Whose hooded, fountain heart once fell in puddles
Round the parched world of Wales and drowned each sun
[Though this for her is a monstrous image blindly
Magnified out of praise ; her death was a still drop ;
She would not have me sinking in the holy
Flood of her heart's fame ; she would lie dumb and deep
And need no druid of her broken body].
But I, Ann's bard on a raised hearth, call all
The seas to service that her wood-tongued virtue
Babble like a bellbuoy over the hymning heads,
Bow down the walls of the ferned and foxy woods
That her love ring and swing through a brown chapel,
Bless her bent spirit with four, crossing birds.
Her flesh was meek as milk, but this skyward statue
With the wild breast and blessed and giant skull
Is carved from her in a room with a wet window
In a fiercely mourning house in a crooked year.
I know her scrubbed and sour humble hands
Lie with religion in their cramp, her threadbare
Whisper in a damp word, her wits drilled hollow,
Her fist of a face died clenched on a round pain ;
And sculptured Ann is seventy years of stone.
These cloud-sopped, marble hands, this monumental
Argument of the hewn voice, gesture and psalm
Storm me forever over her grave until
The stuffed lung of the fox twitch and cry Love
And the strutting fern lay seeds on the black sill.

DYLAN THOMAS

Drawing by Brenda Chamberlain

The Caseg Broadsheet edition of "After the Funeral", with Brenda Chamberlain's haunting image

was this farm where "the Sabbath rang slowly in the pebbles of the holy streams" but also where Dylan was:

> *young and easy under the apple boughs*
> *about the lilting house as happy as the grass was green.*

The farm provides the setting for the first

Portrait… story "The Peaches", but it is renamed Gorsehill. Dylan describes his arrival there from Swansea:

> The front of the house was a single black shell, and the arched door was the listening ear… I pushed the door open and walked into the passage out of the wind… Then a door at the end of the passage opened; I saw the plates on the shelves, the lighted lamp on the long oil-clothed table, 'Prepare to meet Thy God' knitted over the fire place, the smiling china dogs, the brown stained settle, the grandmother clock, and I ran into the kitchen and into Annie's arms.

Several more stories in *Portrait of the Artist* are set in rural Carmarthenshire. "A Visit to Grandpa's" begins in Llanstephan but ends in Carmarthen town, where the young Thomas and the villagers of Johnstown, go in search of his Grandpa. When they eventually catch up with the eccentric old man he is interrogated sternly:

"And what do you think you are doing on Carmarthen Bridge in the middle of the afternoon… with your best waistcoat and old hat?"

"And where do you think you are going with your old black bag?"

Grandpa replies, "I am going to Llangadock to be buried".

"But you aren't dead yet, Dai Thomas."

At different times Dylan would stay at a family cottage in Blaen Cwn which is near Llangain. In later years his parents moved there, and on occasions he and Caitlin would be forced to take refuge there too, but it was not a happy place for them. In November 1934 Dylan writes to Geoffrey Grigson the editor of *New Verse*:

> Penniless I retreated from London and penniless I return. I've been staying all over the place… in a cottage in Carmarthenshire, glorying in the name of Blaen Cwm, where I lived on carrots, (no not quite true, I had onions as well).

In 1944 he is there again with Caitlin, and in a letter to Vernon Watkins he describes the place with bitterness:

> Now we're with my mother and father in Blaen Cwm where every-one goes into the pub sideways, & the dogs piss only on the back doors, and there are more unwanted babies shoved up the chimneys than there are used french letters in the offertory boxes.

With war looking inevitable, Dylan was considering registering as a conscientious objector, but after visiting one such tribunal in Carmarthen with Keidrych Rhys, the sight of endless sad young men being asked on what grounds they objected to military service and hearing their sad mumbling replies, "Religious", and then, on being asked what they were prepared to do, all mumbling an even more pathetic, "Nothing", made Dylan realise that he could not face such a tribunal. Dylan described this day and the effect it had on him to Vernon Watkins, who recollects that:

> When Dylan left this court he felt that one door was closed to him, and later, when his own turn came, he confessed to me that he had signed for the army, but as a "never-fighter".

Wales, Issue 1

Keidrych Rhys would become a good friend; Dylan even managed to turn up as best man when Keidrych married the modernist poet Lynette Roberts. Dylan described the event in a letter to Desmond Hawkins:

> Keidrych has got married to a fantastic but pleasant girl – Dylan drank 41 pints of beer on the wedding day and didn't get up for two days afterwards; local (Welsh) colour.

Surely another example of Dylan's macho hyperbole.

Keidrych was a poet himself but his real talents and lasting legacy were his skill as an editor and publisher. He was born William Ronald Rees Jones 1915, just a year after Dylan, but changed his name when he began to consider a career as a poet. After his marriage and throughout the 1940s he lived at Llanybri and later at Penybont farm, Llangadog, and during this time his only book of poems *The Van Pool* was published in 1942. But it was as editor of the great Anglo-Welsh literary periodical *Wales* that he made his name. He started it – with Dylan's help and support – in 1937. Each one of the first series of 10 issues (issue 11 was a wartime broadsheet) was truly remarkable and Dylan was a ubiquitous contributor, offering important unpublished poems and prose, and his books were reviewed and commented upon as they appeared. His prose piece "Prologue to an Adventure" was the opening piece in the first number, and Dylan was named as co-editor of two issues.

When Keidrych started a second series of the magazine in 1943, Dylan was once again a regular contributor. Sometime later Keidrych would establish

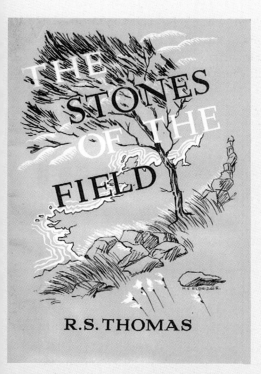

The Druid Press edition of R S Thomas's first book

Aeronwy, who was then ten and away at school in England. The letter is warm and kind and very poignant, and his news is that:

> Mummie's going to Carmarthen tomorrow, which is Wednesday, to buy some things for you, and I'm going to the dentist to scream the house down...

The county town, Carmarthen, was, and still is, a thriving market town, set on the river Towy, and it lays claim to being the oldest town in Wales. It is dominated by a huge Germanic chateau-style building, the County Hall, designed in 1935 by Sir Percy Thomas. It has always had a busy and bustling weekly farmers' market. During the different periods that Dylan lived in Laugharne, Carmarthen was where he and Caitlin went to shop, go to the cinema and enjoy The Boar's Head.

his own press in Carmarthen – The Druid Press which had offices above a shop at 121 Lammas Street just along from The Boar's Head Hotel, handy because this was Dylan's favourite pub in the town. The press never published anything by Dylan but can boast of publishing the first book by one of Wales's other great poets R S Thomas, whose first collection, *The Stones of the Field*, came out in 1946.

Just a few weeks before his death in New York, Dylan wrote the only surviving letter to his daughter

The Boar's Head

Lammas Street, Carmarthen

DYLAN AND CAITLIN liked visiting Carmarthen on Wednesday, the weekly market day, when the pubs were open all hours. Caitlin explained why:

> Every Wednesday we put on our best clothes and caught the bus into Carmarthen for market. This was where we got all our china, blankets and nice clothes for Llewelyn… I liked the atmosphere of market day, all the colours and people pushing and bustling. We would go in together, and then meet up at the *Whore's Bed* (as The Boar's Head was known to everyone in town). It was a good day because on the market day the pubs of Carmarthen stay open all day. By the time I met up with Dylan again, he was always at the centre of a crowd; within two minutes he seemed to know everyone in the pub.

On one market day Vernon Watkins' sister Dot met up with the Thomases in Carmarthen quite by chance. In her *Memoir of Vernon Watkins* she recalls the typically profligate occasion in some detail:

> I was walking along Carmarthen High St. sometime in about 1940 when I ran into Dylan and Caitlin, who had come into town to cash a cheque for 8 guineas, payment from Cyril Connolly for a poem in, I think, *Horizon*. Dylan was gleeful. "We're going to pay off the butcher and the baker," he said, "and have a snack at The Boar to celebrate."
>
> But they passed a dress maker's window in which a Hollywood-cheesecake gold bathing-suit was on display. (Swimming costumes and hats were the only clothes that you could buy without coupons). Caitlin was rapturous.
>
> "I've got to have that, Dylan," she said."My old one is in rags." Dylan tried to put her off. "I like the rags," Dylan said. "You look glorious in them." But Caitlin wheedled and coaxed, and inevitably Dylan was soon leaving the bank and handing over to her a crisp £5 note for her to make her purchase. The rest of the money went in The Boar on a sit-down lunch with beer and a whiskey for Caitlin and a sherry for Dot.
>
> Dot tried desperately to say the lunch was her treat, but Dylan wouldn't allow it. "There isn't enough left to pay for a tube of vaseline," he said, "so the butcher and the baker will have to wait a bit longer." Dylan was quite resigned, and Caitlin of course was ecstatic.

Dylan and Caitlin were later to be back in The Boar with Vernon and Gwen. The Thomases had their rather frisky young son Llewelyn – Vernon's god-child – with them. Gwen later describes the embarrassing episode:

> Vernon's attitude to Llewelyn was of wary reverence; he took his duties very seriously. He sent money when he could, always remembered Christmas and birthday presents, and, when he wrote poems for or about Llewelyn, the payments were faithfully remitted to Laugharne.

One such poem written in 1943 to commemorate Llewelyn's second birthday was called *Llewelyn's Chariot* and it offers a vision of the child as an angelic Greek god. It ends:

Till naked you stand, gold-fleeced, shaping a shell
All seas to your colour, Llewelyn, child above price.

But that particular day, young Llewelyn was far from angelic! He upset the local farmers just by being there but, when he spotted a mouse scampering across the floor he took up a wild chase, jumping over chairs and tables and sending precious pints flying. Gwen describes Llewelyn:

Running among the crowded tables, chanting and knocking glasses and elbows.

The locals were furious and the landlord had no choice; he ejected the party from the pub in no uncertain terms. It was the only occasion when Gwen and Vernon had been thrown out of anywhere. Gwen has never forgotten Dylan, so annoyed at having a good drink spoiled, cursing as they were ushered out, and paraphrasing Vernon's poem ruefully, "Llewelyn, not 'child above price' – Llewelyn, child below MICE!"

The Boar's Head remained Dylan's landmark of choice. In 1952, when Dylan was arranging to give a talk at the local college it was this pub that was to serve as the liaison point:

I don't know what time I'll be getting to Carmarthen so I wonder if anyone could pick me up at the Boar's Head at about 6.30. That would give us time for a surreptitious drink before going on to the College.

(from an unpublished letter dated October 1952)

At the college Dylan had a good, but somewhat unlikely, friend in the Rev Professor Stephens, who was a theology lecturer. Dylan would often call on him to chat about poetry and philosophy. On the death of Dylan's father, Stephens sent Dylan and his mother a letter of condolence. Dylan replied with a letter which has echoes of his great poem *Do Not Go Gentle Into That Good Night*:

> My father was in great pain and distress at the end, and nearly blind; but though we wished him peace and rest, his death was a terrible loss to us all.

When the Rev Stephens retired in 1954, a colleague, the accomplished artist John Wright, presented him with a fine pen and wash portrait of Dylan, inscribed on the verso, "in memory or a great Welsh poet and thinker".

The Boar's Head also features at the start of the sad final chapter in Dylan's life. It was there that he took his last drink in West Wales. On the evening of October 8th, 1953, the night before he and Caitlin were due to leave for London, where Caitlin would send him off on his last fatal trip to America, they decided to go into Carmarthen to see a film. As became ominously clear in the next weeks, Dylan was not in good health. By chance, Dylan's family doctor – Dr David Hughes of St Clears – was sitting in the row in front. Before the film started, Caitlin leaned over and told him of her concerns over Dylan's health, especially as he was off to America. The doctor offered to pick them up in his car when the film ended and

John Wright's fine portrait of Dylan

Dylan Thomas

Wright '52

take them to his surgery to give Dylan a check-up.

We can only speculate on just what the doctor would have discovered and diagnosed – for when the lights went up Dylan was nowhere to be seen. He had crept out and made his way to The Boar's Head for a nightcap and to escape the good doctor's attentions. The doctor went home without seeing him and in the morning Dylan and Caitlin left for London via a stopover in Swansea. Within three weeks Dylan would be lying dead in St Vincent's Hospital in New York.

The Boar's Head today

The Boar's Head Hotel is still a large and fine establishment offering good beer, food and accommodation.

Laugharne
Carmarthenshire

The fairies inhabiting these islands are said to have regularly attended the markets at Laugharne. They made their purchases without speaking, laid down their money and departed, always leaving the exact sum required, which they seemed to know, without asking the price of anything. Sometimes they were invisible, but they were often seen, by sharp-eyed persons.
– from Wirt Sykes, *British Goblins*, published 1880

ON HIS FIRST VISIT to Laugharne in 1934, Dylan wrote to Pamela Hansford Johnson describing the place as:

the strangest town in Wales… the nearest approach under the sun to a Stygian borough.

The woodcut and quote above, from Wirt Sykes's rare study of Welsh goblins and fairy folk, would seem to suggest that Dylan too, experienced something peculiar in the town!

Although Dylan Thomas was born and lived in Swansea for half of his pitifully short life (he died just days after his 39th birthday), for many people he is more often associated with Laugharne. This may be because of the worldwide popularity of his great radio play *Under Milk Wood*, which exists in many languages and editions; is on records and CDs; has been filmed with Burton, Taylor and O'Toole; has been turned into an animated film and is performed endlessly in school halls, tin sheds and theatres around the world. Many people have come to know Laugharne, and indeed Wales, through the play, and they know that it was partly inspired by, based on, and written in Laugharne. The town has come to represent Dylan's mythical "Llareggub"(spell it backwards to get Dylan's naughty joke).

Add to this the spectacular location and appearance of Dylan's final Laugharne home, The Boathouse, which Dylan decribes as his "seashaken house on a breakneck of rocks", and you have a perfect literary tourist's destination. The Boathouse is now conserved and open to the public as a place of pilgrimage. It functions as both museum and tea room and is currently developing a programme of occasional literary and musical events as well.

Laugharne is a charming place to visit, with other attractions besides those associated with Dylan Thomas. James A Davies writes:

> When Dylan Thomas came to Laugharne it was – and to some extent still is – an isolated, atmospheric, somewhat down at heel, and rather eccentric place… In a fiercely Welsh-speaking area, but, with its Portreeve and Georgian buildings, [it] is an English-speaking enclave, a beautiful eccentric place for a Swansea man with little Welsh, and rural leanings.

Dylan's first official biographer, Constantine Fitzgibbon, wrote that Laugharne:

fitted Dylan like a single, eccentric, tattered glove.

Note how the word "eccentric" keeps cropping up! Vernon Watkins sums it all up nicely when he writes:

> Just before the war I stayed with Dylan frequently in Laugharne. The peace and beauty of this small sea-town… a fishing village at the end of the world represented for him the last refuge of life and sanity in a nightmare world.

Laugharne was the title and subject of Dylan's last radio feature. It was broadcast live to an audience of locals which included Caitlin Thomas. With a cruel irony it was during this evening that the local policeman delivered a telegram to her informing her that Dylan was very ill in New York. But in his broadcast, Dylan is still celebrating the town in all its eccentric glory, describing it as:

> This timeless, beautiful, barmy (both spellings) town… a legendary lazy little black-magical bedlam by the sea.

Dylan's first visit was with the Welsh writer Glyn Thomas in 1934; they both had family in Llanstephan and came across the estuary to Laugharne by ferry. In 1936 he was back in town successfully fighting for, courting and winning the love of Caitlin Macnamara, and in 1938, Dylan brought her as his wife to Laugharne to live in the appropriately-named Eros in Gosport Street. Sadly the romance of the place ended with the name; Eros was a damp tiny cottage with no bathroom and an outside lavatory. Writing to the poet and critic Henry Treece, Dylan described it bluntly:

I must warn you that our cottage is pokey and ugly, four rooms like stained boxes in a workman's and fisherman's row, with a garden leading down to mud and sea, that our living & cooking is rough, that you bathe or go dirty.

However the same letter goes upbeat when he gets onto a favourite topic:

I hope you like drinking, because I do very much and when I have money I don't stop. There are three good pubs and the best bottled mild… and no prohibitive drinking hours.

Writing to his American publisher James Laughlin in 1938 from Eros, Dylan describes Laugharne as "a very odd town", but he goes on to recommend it as:

a good place, undiscovered by painters, and, because the sea is mostly mud and nobody knows when the water will come in or go out or where it comes from anyway, with few sprinkling trippers or picnickers. It's a sociable place too, and I like that, with good pubs and little law and no respect.

He and Caitlin would suffer Eros for just three months, its sordid conditions and the early morning ordeal of having to trek down the hill to get water from the public tap. Dylan was often seen staggering along, bucket in hand, dressed in his pyjamas and overcoat, so he was relieved to move his now pregnant wife up the hill to a much bigger house, Sea View.

They were happy there and had room to accommodate a stream of visitors, and Dylan's writing was going well. They probably would have stayed but mounting debts to local tradesmen drove them back to Caitlin's mother in Hampshire. After Llewelyn was born they were back in Sea View, having placated their local creditors, but by July 1940 the debts had mounted up again – and once more they were forced to leave.

The couple and their young family – Aeronwy was born in 1943 – spent the war years as virtual itinerants, staying wherever seemed safest and offered free or cheap living. They would have come back to Laugharne in 1944, but failing to find anywhere suitable, they moved to New Quay instead. It was to be 1949 before they managed to get back to Laugharne when yet another of Dylan's benefactors stepped in to help.

Margaret Taylor was the wife of the historian A J P Taylor, who did not in any way share his wife's enthusiasm; he thought Dylan was a loathsome sponger. But Margaret was besotted and she helped find The Boathouse, the "house on stilts" that sat under the sea-cliff, a manageable walk from Browns. She paid £3,000 for it and allowed the Thomases to live there virtually rent-free. Dylan was genuinely grateful to have been delivered of such an idyllic house. He wrote to Margaret on May 11th, 1949 thanking her:

for this place I love and where I want to work… this is *it*: the place, the house, the workroom, the time… All I shall write in this water and tree room on the cliff, every word will be my thanks to you. You have given me a life. And now I am going to live it.

Sadly this wish was to extend for little more than five years.

Laugharne boasts a remarkable system of local government; Laugharne Corporation is the UK's last surviving medieval corporation. It was established in 1290, and is presided over by a portreeve, who gets to wear an elaborate chain of office made up of solid gold seashells and he oversees regular meetings and ceremonial gatherings. Customs include the Common Walk, which occurs every three years and involves a long trek around the boundaries of corporation lands. A highlight of the official Laugharne year was the portreeve's annual lecture. By 1953 Dylan was considered enough of a local to be invited to be the honoured speaker, however his response has a sad poignancy:

Dear Mr Roberts:

Thank you very much indeed for your kind invitation to me to attend the Port-Reeve's Annual Breakfast this coming Sunday. Unfortunately, I am going to London today & from there to America, and will have to miss the pleasure of the Breakfast. I am very sorry, but I wish you a very pleasant Sunday morning & the best of wishes over the coming year. Yours sincerely:

Dylan Thomas

It was on this trip to America that Dylan died in St Vincent's Hospital, New York.

The 1951 UK Census records that the town consisted of just 313 private households. Around 180 of these had no piped water, 162 shared a toilet with another household and 210 had no fixed bath. The township had 1,010 residents, which included the Thomases, their three children in The Boathouse and Dylan's parents, Florence and DJ, across from Browns in The Pelican. But despite these apparently unattractive statistics it is worth noting that Laugharne has a rich literary history both before and after Dylan Thomas lived there. It begins with Jeremy Taylor, a chaplain to Charles I and author of two books *Holy Living* (1650) and *Holy Dying* (1651). Between 1776 and 1782 the great proto-feminist Mary Wollstonecraft lived with her father on a farm on the outskirts of the town and much later her equally celebrated daughter, Mary Shelley, author of the gothic horror classic, *Frankenstein* (1818), is said to have stayed in Laugharne.

The nineteenth-century English poet Walter Savage Landor, who lived in Tenby and Swansea, became a visitor and the more famous English Romantic poet Samuel Taylor Coleridge paid a visit when Wales was beginning to attract its first gentlemen tourists.

The First World War poet and prose writer Edward Thomas stayed in Laugharne in 1911, in a boarding house in Victoria Street, and he completed his biography of George Borrow while there. A couple of years later he set some of his only novel, *The Happy-Go-Lucky Morgans*, in the town, which he loosely disguised as "Abercorran".

In the 30s and 40s Welsh novelists – husband and wife team Charles Morgan and Hilda Vaughan – were visitors to the town and Hilda used Laugharne as the setting for her novel *Harvest Home* (1936). Charles Morgan stayed in Castle House as the guest of another of Laugharne's literary residents, Richard Hughes. Hughes was a very well connected playwright, poet and novelist whose most famous book *A High Wind in Jamaica* was made into a highly successful film. Hughes did much of his writing in the small gazebo, perched high on the ruined castle walls looking out over the estuary.

With excellent timing Dylan and Caitlin had arrived in Laugharne and they were befriended by Hughes and his wife Frances. Hughes finished his novel *In Hazard* in the late 30s, so he vacated the gazebo, thus allowing Dylan Thomas to move in and write most of his collection of semi-autobiographical short stories that became his book *Portrait of the Artist as a Young Dog*. When it was published in 1940, Dylan inscribed a copy to Hughes who was known as "Diccon" and his wife Frances, in gratitude for letting him use such a wonderful writing room.

Hughes was always a very kind, generous, and long-suffering friend and supporter of Dylan and Caitlin while they were Laugharne. But Dylan knew his place in the town's literary hierarchy, he wrote a note about himself for the periodical *Life and Letters* saying of Laugharne:

> Its literary values are firmly established: Richard Hughes lives in a castle at the top of the hill; I live in a shed at the bottom.

More recently the somewhat eccentric modernist writer Lynette Roberts, who was once married to Dylan's friend Keidrych Rhys, lived in a caravan near St Martin's Church. Her book of wartime poems *Gods With Stainless Ears*, which Faber published, has become something of a secret classic.

Kingsley Amis moved down to Laugharne to

Augustus John's portrait of his friend Richard "Diccon" Hughes

write his Booker Prize-winning novel, *The Old Devils* (1986). An often bitter and cruel critic of both Dylan and Caitlin's writings and lifestyle, it had shocked many people when Amis joined his drinking pal, Stuart Thomas, as a trustee of The Dylan Thomas Trust. Stuart was a Swansea solicitor and school friend of Dylan's who subsequently acted for the Thomases – Dylan, Caitlin, and for Dylan's parents, throughout their lives. As for Amis, his sojourn in Laugharne seemed to have a positive effect on his work as *The Old Devils* is generally considered a late return to form some 30 years after he shot to fame with *Lucky Jim*. The novel includes a character, a poet Brydan, who is used by Amis to lampoon Dylan and satirise the cult of personality that grew up around him.

Recently Canadian writer Margaret Atwood included an interesting story in her collection *Dancing Girls and Other Stories* (1977) and is titled "The Grave of the Famous Poet". Although it is a fictional love story about two travellers, the grave in question is that of Dylan Thomas and it is obvious from the text that Atwood had visited Laugharne.

Although there is no doubt that Dylan was very fond of Laugharne, if it suited him he could be less than flattering to the town. After his first visit to

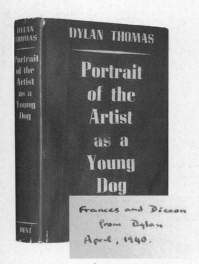

First edition of *Dylan's* Portrait stories inscribed to Richard Hughes

the States in 1950 he wrote of long and wonderful, sometimes scurrilous, sometimes scatological, verse letter, back to some good friends he stayed with in Greenwich Village, New York. Lloyd Frankenberg was a poet and critic and his partner Loren McIver was a highly regarded New York painter. Lloyd had been involved in arranging some of Dylan's first readings in New York and the couple introduced Dylan to the best and most interesting Greenwich Village artists, writers and intellectuals. By way of some kind of "quid pro quo" Dylan sent them a long and highly wrought verse letter, in parts of which he is rather harsh on Laugharne. Dylan starts gently, describing it as a:

> cockles and mussels town …pretty as a stricture town by the eely oily, licking sea.

But he continues in a rather different and more gothic vein, this sea is:

> full of fish that taste like feet and feet that taste like fur.

Then he warms to his task and gets quite carried away; Laugharne is where:

> welcome is botched on the mat of the excrementious town hall with blood and spinach …excreta whirls through the window, turdy as Venice.

And then "under a bathwater sky" live "goitered scraggy swans", "cow pouncing owls" and "a whiskey whiskered seal wet barking virgin with spurs on her teats" that "gives birth to a mole in the main street".

And where the inhabitants, all "nine hundred gabies", enjoy a full and ordered life:

Today we hunt babies…
Tomorrow's the day for the circumcision of birds…
And on "cannibal Sunday" they all:
hope the vicar's sweet!

This depiction is getting closer to *Milk Wood*'s Llareggub! And it is *Under Milk Wood* that really puts Laugharne on the literary map. Although New Quay gave Dylan the beginnings of an idea which grew out of his broadcast *Quite Early One Morning,* he later writes about the work being:

An extravagant play… about a day's life in a small town in a never-never Wales.

He goes on to explain:

But out of my working, however vainly, on it, came the idea of Llareggub… Out of it came the idea that I write a piece, a play an impression for voices, an entertainment out of the darkness, of the town I live in, and to write it simply and warmly and comically with lots of movement and varieties of moods, so that at many levels, through sight and speech, description and dialogue, evocation and parody, you come to know the town as an inhabitant of it… never judge nor condemn but explain and make strangely simple and simply strange.

And to his Swansea friend John Ormond Thomas, he writes:

a radio play I am writing has Laugharne, though not by name, as its setting, I do so want to pay a tribute to Laugharne.

And judging by the play's continued success and popularity with drama groups and audiences worldwide, Dylan seems to have achieved his goal (as I am writing this an e-mail has just arrived telling me a new version, involving original sea shanties, is about to be staged in Louisiana during the New Orleans Fringe Theatre Festival!).

Today the locals are charming and welcoming and very proud of their town. One of them, Bob Stevens, a local farmer and councillor, has recently established a well-marked and splendid walk, The Dylan Thomas Birthday Walk. It is based around Thomas's *Poem in October,* which recounts a walk up Sir John's Hill that Dylan enjoyed on the day he turned 30. Bob Stevens has installed a series of benches at key points along the two-mile trail and inscribed each with lines from the poem that reflect the views, and alongside are explanatory information panels. And as an added bonus, lucky visitors who complete the walk on their birthday and present ID at various local pubs and cafés can claim a free birthday pint or a portion of fish and chips from Laugharne's famous chippie; and it is best to eat them on the benches across the road by the castle while reading the poem again:

It was my thirtieth
Year to heaven stood there
then in the summer noon
leaved with October blood.
O may my heart's truth

Still be sung
On this high hill in a year's turning.

The castle is now one of Cadw's properties and is open to the public in its own right and it is currently being revamped. Another recent and very worthwhile addition to the Laugharne calendar and landscape is the annual Laugharne Weekend, an arts festival held in the spring which is deliberately small-scale and means that visitors and townspeople get to rub shoulders with artists and performers. *The Guardian* describes it as the:

> wondrous Welsh literary arts festival set in Dylan Thomas country.

A rare snap of Dylan and family on the Laugharne ferry

The Laugharne Weekend always has a louche line-up with a leaning towards current Welsh music and literature together with big-name and interesting headliners – past festivals have hosted the great American poet and songwriter Patti Smith, Ray Davies of the Kinks and Mick Jones of The Clash. The festival almost wilfully avoids too much Dylan Thomas but he does creep into the more unusual and eclectic events. All events take place in clubs, churches and halls, tiny and intimate venues, which adds to the special atmosphere of the whole weekend. It is worth mentioning that during 2014 – Dylan's centenary – there will be four Laugharne Weekend festivals spaced throughout the year.

Perhaps we should all heed the prophesy of the old Welsh wizard Merlin:

> Kidwelly was, Carmarthen is, and Laugharne will be the greatest city of the three.

Browns Hotel

ON THE AFTERNOON of May 21st, 1934, on his first ever visit to Laugharne, Dylan Thomas sat down for tea in Browns Hotel. Of all the pubs featured in this book, Browns must be the most famous, and most visited, for its connections with Dylan Thomas. When literary pilgrims make it to Laugharne, and they make it in their thousands from all over the world; they want to explore the town, to look round at the twelfth-century castle ruins, to visit the Boathouse, maybe enjoy the wonderful Birthday Walk up and over St John's Hill, – but most of all they want a drink in Browns! And thankfully once again they can – because after being closed for too long, Browns has reopened its doors as a fine boutique hotel.

The old hotel stopped taking guests in 1959, six years after Thomas's death, and the bar finally closed in 2006. After a £2m renovation, it is now fully refurbished, but not over-restored, and still offers the same fine bar that Dylan loved as his second Laugharne home, but also offers splendid accommodation in boutique-style rooms that would surely make Dylan's hair curl even tighter!

Browns Hotel is situated in King Street, close to the eighteenth-century market house, the Town Hall and the castle ruins. It was built in 1752 as a private house before becoming a hotel in the 1800s. The bar is now listed by Cadw and known locally as The Browns (the apostrophe vanished some years ago). When Dylan Thomas lived in Laugharne it soon became his favourite pub and he wrote of how he would sit in the corner "mouldering" and writing at a wrought-iron window table or playing cards, but all the while listening to the conversations of the locals that swirled around the bar, for these would make the raw materials for his radio play *Under Milk Wood*.

The pub was kept by Ivy Thomas, and her husband Ebie – and they both befriended Dylan. The Williamses were a ubiquitous Laugharne family with fingers in many pies. They owned Sea View and let it to Dylan during his earlier sojourn in the town, and they also owned The Pelican, a large house opposite Browns, which Dylan rented for his ageing parents so they were close by, and he could take care of them. Ivy was a constant source of local stories and gossip, much of which would inform and reappear in the pages of *Under Milk Wood*. Ivy was very fond of Dylan and extended him credit, fed him, spoiled him, and played cards with him. An indication of Dylan's fondness and respect for Ivy comes across in this account of an altercation written by the artist Frances Hughes, the wife of the novelist Richard Hughes:

> Dylan's fight with Bill was successful to the point of Billy being in bed for three weeks, mostly from his bad knee. It was not a very short one either. It appears they were all out for the day with Dr Rolley Thomas, and then Billy was rude to Ivy in the bar, and she sent him out, and on the doorstep,

he knocked her flat onto her back in the doorway. She was full of refined indignation, still adjuring him, "Get out of my house". Dylan protested and Billy knocked him head over heels out into the road; by the time he got up, two of Billy's friends had hurried him away, but just after came Dylan back and met him at our gates, and there were fine words passed, and then a big fight, and Dylan got hit in the face, but he got at Billy, and after got him on the ground, and then the brothers came all at Dylan, so he expected destruction, but Old Tom spoke up that Billy began it. So Tudor pulled him from under Dylan and carried him off quite dangling with his legs bent back under him, which Dylan said made a good END, only that he had been having a good time bashing Billy's head on the pavement… Besides that the policeman shook Dylan's hand in the street and said it was done fine.

Dylan was also good friends with Ivy's husband Ebie and they shared many escapades, which also sound reminiscent of episodes in *Under Milk Wood*. In a letter to his friends Bill and Helen McAlpine Dylan writes:

Early this week, Ebie, laying his pistol down, and I, went to Whitland Mart and bought three geese & a turkey… All alive. The buying took fifteen minutes, just after lunch, but, oddly, we didn't return till midnight, the birds in the boot savage and famished. Now they all live on the lawn at back of Brown's, leering into the kitchen. We had a farmerish day, and came back covered in manure, slapping little sticks against our thighs, talking turkey and a lot of cock. Ebie didn't get up till teatime the next day, and then rushed off to be given medicine by his fancy woman, the chemist. Next day he didn't get up at all.

The aside, that Ebie will be "laying the pistol down" is a reference to a 1943 country and western song *Pistol Packin' Mama* and was no doubt prompted by Ebie's infatuation with the Wild West; Dylan would refer to him as "Texan Ebie". Writing home to Caitlin from America, Dylan urges her to:

tell Ebie, "… Sunday I fly to Montana, where the cowboys are, thousands of them", and he adds that he is going to bring Ebie back "something cowboy".

Dylan called in the pub most mornings, often for tea and some breakfast, and he drank there most nights when he was in Laugharne, often accompanied by Caitlin, so much so that he would give the hotel phone number as his own. When a Neath man, Peter Davies, wanted to visit, Dylan wrote to him:

you can leave a message for me at Laugharne 13: the pub.

In a 1938 letter to his Swansea pal, John Prichard, who was planning a visit in the summer he wrote:

You know how to get to Laugharne, don't you… Drop in at Brown's Hotel & buy a Felinfoel and ask where we live: they know.

By 1948, Dylan was such a fixture in the pub that he had also became a "fitting"; writing about Laugharne to his Swansea friend John Ormond Thomas, he tells him:

my photograph, even, looking repellent, is hung on the walls of Brown's Hotel.

Nora Summers' photograph of Dylan and Caitlin in Laugharne

Most mornings Dylan would go to Browns to catch up with Ivy and to start the daily crossword puzzle, before going across the road to finish it with his father. He would study the racing pages, as he had developed a minor addiction to backing horses – probably a desperate "get-rich-quick scheme" which never came off. Phil Cross, the landlord down at The Cross Inn, also speaks of Dylan's fascination, and mild obsession, with horse-racing and he talks of them having a regular little flutter. Because of Dylan's always dire financial situation, his bets were always going to be minimal but some of the motivation was surely that "clutching at straws" dream of instant riches should an intricate accumulator bet romp home.

But there was, I think, a little more to this. Although both Phil and Brinnin talk of Dylan poring over the racing pages, it was as much for the joy he got from the surrealist juxtapositions and verbal music that the names and lists of runners threw up. I am sure his bets were governed more by his delight in a name than the nag's current form. And this would seem to be borne out by this spontaneous "found" poem which he scrawled as an addition to a postcard that a friend was sending from Laugharne. The card, dating from the early 50s features, on the front, a view of King Street and Browns Hotel with The Pelican opposite.

On the other side is the sender's brief message, followed by Dylan's "poem", made up of the bizarre juxtaposition of the curious names of horses he has backed – the fact they are referred to as "camels" would suggest they were not the winners he had hoped for!

Dylan's spontaneous poem on a postcard from Laugharne

Running Water and Nuts,
French Bounty and Knuckles,
D'Angelo and Chammie,
Belby Belby Belby,
Jackmil and Ambiguity
are some of the Camels we have mounted.

Dylan was also very happy to welcome and receive guests in Browns and his visitors included North Country poet and writer, Henry Treece, Swansea artists Fred Janes, and Mervyn Levy, Ceri Richards and Augustus John, and Dylan's best literary friend, Vernon Watkins who visited with his wife Gwen, and Tenby-born painter Augustus John.

In her book *My Father's Places: A Portrait of Childhood* (2009), Dylan's daughter Aeronwy recalls, as a schoolgirl, seeing the "unmistakable" silhouettes of her father and grandfather sitting in the pub's bay window, studying folded newspapers. She also remembered Dylan playing traditional pub games shove-halfpenny and skittles and describes how landlady Ivy Williams would cook huge casserole lunches and spend much time in the bar gossiping with the men, serving customers and playing cards. She goes on to write of how her father had to be back from his morning trip to Browns by 1pm for a lunch fry-up, before serious afternoon writing began at 2pm in the shed which would last until the early evening when, invariably, her parents would head back to the pub.

In November 1953 Browns was the obvious location for Dylan's wake after his burial at the church. It was, as one would have expected, a lively affair but it is hard these days to pick the bones of truth out of the soup of exaggeration that has been concocted around many of the significant events in Dylan's life. Suffice to say that at some point, and for some unknown reason, Caitlin poured a tray full of fresh pints over poor undeserving Fred Janes. And when, after her death in 1984, Caitlin's body was brought to

Laugharne from Italy for her to be buried alongside Dylan, her wake; another lively affair, was held in Browns.

Browns Hotel today

Following in Dylan Thomas's footsteps, other visitors to Browns have included President Jimmy Carter, Richard Burton, Elizabeth Taylor, Patti Smith, Pierce Brosnan and Mick Jagger. These last two were rumoured to be competing to buy a battered old steel bedstead that the then landlord Tommy Watts was promoting as the Thomases' actual nuptial bed! Browns is rumoured to have been the source of numerous "dartboards that Dylan bulls-eyed", "Lucky pub tables he won card games on" and all manner of other dubious memorabilia.

I was once offered, and urged to buy, the Laugharne hearse that was used to bring Thomas's body from the dockside in Southampton back to Laugharne! On another occasion I was offered a patch of real woodlands near Llandeilo which was being pitched quite seriously as "THE ACTUAL UNDER MILK WOOD" – a claim based solely on two lines from Eli Jenkins's Morning Prayer:

> A tiny dingle is Milk Wood
> By Golden Grove 'neath Grongar

When I naively asked the enthusiastic vendor what I

Dylan and a pal with pints, outside Browns (a hitherto unpublished snapshot)

might do with the woods on offer he assured me that, "people, especially Americans, would pay a fortune to be buried there".

Browns was recently owned for a time by actor Neil Morrissey before being sold in 2006. The new owners have done a grand job in modernising but not spoiling this iconic building. They describe it on their website thus:

> To enter Browns Hotel today is to step back into a memorable, simpler, slower time of reassuring certainties. Its 1940s and 1950s heyday was a time when conversation, community, coffee and cake would regularly set the world to rights. Our hotel thrives on an elegant mix of modern comfort, charming touchstones, Welsh excellence and its warm welcome. Browns Hotel is re-born as a thoroughly contemporary boutique hotel.

It is hard to argue with this, the new-look Browns is a far cry from the rough-and-ready boozer of Thomas's day. Today, instead of Tommy Watts's warm beer and Desperate Dan-style plates of ham, egg and chips, the bar offers local real ales and plates of gourmet Welsh charcuterie. The renovation (overseen by designer Juliet Bragg) has moved away from any kind of themed Dylan-Disneyland, but offers instead a tasteful refit, which attempts a 1940/50s time period, and tries to reflect and recreate the ambience of Laugharne in that decade.

In the reading room there are piles of books by Thomas and his biographers, as well as a plethora of interesting period paraphernalia – lots of vintage cameras and museum-piece record players. Elsewhere, nods to the poet are scarce but telling. A stark, black-and-white image of the writer in the bar, back to the camera, hangs alongside an exhibition of images of Laugharne life on the staircase. The bedrooms are cosy but modern, dominated by huge floor-to-ceiling murals made from blown-up monochrome images of Laugharne in the 50s. Lucky guests can find pocket book editions of Thomas's writings alongside the Gideon Bibles in the bedside cabinets!

The Cross House

LAUGHARNE has a topography that in effect cuts the town in half, and because the two halves are at a different height above sea level, people refer to the "upper town" and "lower town", or "up street" and "down street", and a bit like the East End/West End divide in London, there is an element of snobbery and attitude involved. As you enter Laugharne, the upper town stretches from St Martin's Church down to the castle and then as you progress downwards the area surrounding the muddy estuary is the lower town. So both physically and in attitude, the upper town looks down on the lower town.

However it is the lower town that includes what is the natural focal centre of the town – a sort of village square of reclaimed land, but – being Laugharne – it is more triangular in shape. It is known as The Grist, and in the centre is a fine ancient Celtic cross.

There are many theories about the name. Some believe that there was once a monastery in Laugharne called Christ Church (hence the Celtic cross), while others say that the name derives from a former corn or grist mill which once existed at the mouth of the river Corran, and we must also bear in mind that "Jesus Christ" in Welsh is "Iesu Grist".

Dylan ends a desperate begging letter sent to Augustus John in 1950 with the macabre salutation, "See you on the cross", which Ferris explains in a footnote, is a reference not just to the crucifixion but also a nod to Laugharne's Square and The Cross House pub. Although Dylan lived more in the upper town he was very familiar with this area too; his first house in Laugharne was a tiny cottage Eros in this lower part of the town. Older locals still have memories of Dylan, sitting cradling a beer in The Cross House, writing ideas for new poems and characters on Woodbine cigarette packets, sadly all swept up and thrown away by the fastidious bar staff.

The Cross became one of his favourite Laugharne pubs, as his later 1949 letter to his friend Bill McAlpine (addressed from the "Hut on Hill") indicates. Dylan jokes with Bill about how he is going to delight in announcing the news that Bill has had promotion in his work:

And how glad too will be your age-old friends in the township when, this Saturday night, when I tell them in the great shining bars, the chromium Corporation, and The Cross Club – Dancing to Romaine and her Music.

The Romaine in question was Romaine Richards, the daughter and multi-talented assistant to her father, the landlord of The Cross, Phil Richards, was one of Dylan's closer Laugharne friends, but as Phil was at pains to point out, he knew Dylan:

not as a poet but as a man. You see he was a great friend, a wonderful fellow.

They became friends in the late 1940s when Phil had moved to Laugharne to take on the running of The Cross, and Dylan had moved back to Laugharne and into the Boathouse. Phil would often arrange for a driver to take himself and Dylan off for a day's pub crawling. Phil liked to describe these jollies as "little outings together" which took them off to places like Glanamman or over to Carreg Cennen for bread and cheese in the Cennin Arms. Inevitably they arrived back a little too late and a little too worse for wear, and both received serious tongue-lashings from their long-suffering but feisty spouses. Phil also recalls Dylan being in The Cross with his Irish friend Bill McAlpine… but let's hear Phil tell this particular bit of blarney:

Oh I'll tell you about a pig now. A little feller, a little Irishman, called Bill McAlpine, had a few drinks in the morning here, and he thought he'd have a walk. Not a lot of beer, mind you. What we drunk was very, very small, but felt like a walk, and we got as far as Billy Maelor's place and we seen a pig in the road, and Dylan said, "Damn it all," he said, "I'd like to buy that," he says. Right – we'll buy it. We buy the pig. Looking for money, Billy Maelor wanted fifteen pounds for the pig. And we found seven quid – Bill McAlpine, meself, and Dylan – we found seven. And I think it took us about three hours, bringing the pig – is it three hundred yards. Maybe it's a little more… We had a rope on the back leg and Bill McAlpine was pushing him and Dylan pulling as well. And I was a bit dubious, afraid of course. Anyway eventually we arrived home at The Cross House. Now, food. We had no food for the pig. So Billy, Billy Maelor comes chasing after us with a little bag, "for his feed in the morning." First thing, like. Now, Dylan said, "We've got to name the thing. What shall we call him? Er – we'll call him Wallace."

[Dylan] used to come down every morning and look over the wall. Old Wallace was doing very very well… my wife looked after it. Anyway Wallace grew up to be a wonderful thing… after about nine months he turned about to be about fourteen or fifteen stone. And anyway the execution come on a Saturday morning – I'll never forget it. Once Dylan had come down and the Butcher here, killing the pig in the garage here. Everything ready, we'd been boiling water and the butcher come, and Dylan and I were in the front room. And we were like this holding our ears, for the last scream, for the last scream like, you see. Had a pint or two again, paid the Butcher and the day passed.

Well Dylan had to go, leaving for London soon afterwards – he went to Camden Town. He was coming back for Christmas, and we, we'll have Wallace back for our Christmas meal. Huge pig… It was killed, yes, yes. And salted… He turned out to be a beauty. Beauty. Monster.

Could this be the inspiration for Dylan's Butcher Beynon character in *Under Milk Wood*?

Mr Beynon in butcher's bloodied apron, springheels down Coronation Street, a finger, not his own in his mouth.

It is no wonder Dylan would later write back to Caitlin from America that he intended to "buy a shirt for Phil"! Dylan's daughter Aeronwy has also written her memories of this incident. It was her unfortunate job as a young ten-year-old to collect and carry the pails of waste food from the Boathouse, and from her grandparents in The Pelican, down to The Cross to feed the pig. And she recalls:

Whenever Dylan visited The Cross House, he and Phil would lean on the sty and argue; "My half is making better progress than yours".

Apart from bringing Phil gifts back from America, Dylan would also patronise his pub when his American friend and erstwhile tour manager, John Malcolm Brinnin, visited Dylan and Caitlin to discuss further reading tours. Brinnin visited, with his partner Bill Read, in the summer of 1951. Dylan met them at Carmarthen station, with the Laugharne chauffeur Billy Williams in tow, to drive them back to Laugharne. This is Brinnin's recollections of that first visit:

Entering the village at the beginning of the long Welsh twilight, we drove through crooked streets lined with grey stuccoed houses, caught sight of the jaunty little town clock-tower with its weathercock sitting in the wind, passed the wooden turnstile leading to the castle, and stopped in the seaside bottom of the village at The Cross House, the pub where Caitlin was to join us for a drink… we found the little pub beginning to fill up with villagers and Welsh song, then first notes of which struck us as curiously off-key.

Through the din of rising choruses, Caitlin arrived… someone passed around a jar of pickled cockles and we ate these with our bitters as the pub became more crowded, smoky and boisterous. A grimy man in a cap began to sing the Welsh national anthem. This was taken up all around and we departed The Cross House on a loud cracked crescendo of Welsh pride.

It seems that, for Brinnin, Wales did not live up to its "Land of Song" sobriquet and he would not agree with *Milk Wood*'s Rev Eli Jenkins's exhortation, "Praise the Lord! We are a musical nation." And it only got worse for the cultured and somewhat effete American as he writes of his return visit to the pub:

A few hours later Dylan and Bill came to take me to The Cross House... as we drank in rather minimal cordiality in The Cross House, the customary Saturday night song fest raged about us. We bore it until our eardrums ached, then said good nights and walked back to the village.

Brinnin was more likely to agree with *Milk Wood*'s Mrs Organ Morgan, who complains of her husband Mr Organ Morgan:

It's organ, organ, all the time with him.

And she wails:

Oh, I'm a martyr to Music.

Brinnin had two people with him on his visit, one was his friend, the photographer Rollie McKenna, and the other, his partner Bill Read, an American academic. Read would later publish a very good pictorial biography of Dylan – *The Days of Dylan Thomas* (1965), which featured Rollie's fine photographs and her selection of most of the best images of the poet. In 1957, four years after Dylan's death Bill Read gave a talk called *A Visit to Laugharne* on Boston University's radio station, which offers a slightly different perspective to Brinnin's account:

We drove through the main street, past the town hall with its bell-topped tower, past the castle, and down to the edge of the sea where we stopped at "Phil's pub" officially known as The Cross Keys (sic). There I could see that the town was not without pride in the success of its local boy: prominently displayed on a wall of the pub was a large

framed photograph of Dylan at the age of seventeen or so – a childish oval face, large round eyes under a mass of uncombed ringlets. This delicate creature in a homespun sweater was an image of freshness and innocence. Dylan himself, now thirty-seven, had the same shining eyes as he stood beside it, even more tousled hair, and a vastly more mature and heavy face.

Caitlin adds a final word on The Cross when she writes about Dylan's father, D J Thomas, who, with his wife Florrie, had moved into a house, The Pelican, opposite Browns Hotel in the upper town. Although D J would just have to step across the road to Browns if he fancied a drink, he chose not to. Caitlin writes:

In those last years, the only thing he (DJ) did outside his home was occasionally to walk down the hill to The Cross House for a couple of pints, and he only went there because he knew that we would either be at Brown's Hotel or the Corporation Arms. This was his only real pleasure, and I think he quite enjoyed an argument with Phil Richards, the landlord.

The Cross House today

Today The Cross House is a thriving pub, popular with locals and visitors alike. It has a Captain Cat's Bar and Polly Garter's lounge, after characters in *Under Milk Wood*, and serves good food and real ales.

West Wales

W EST WALES for Dylan Thomas was Cardiganshire and Pembrokeshire. His ancestors on both his mother and father's side were from Carmarthenshire stock but David John Thomas, Dylan's father, had ventured further west to Aberystwyth to study English. He graduated with a first class honours degree in 1899, a quite remarkable achievement, for in that year only two degrees of this, the highest class, were awarded throughout the whole of the University of Wales. Dylan himself spent a weekend in the town in 1934, with his new friend, the novelist and short story writer and Cardiff schoolmaster Glyn Jones. The purpose of their visit was to call on, and pay homage to, the local famous, and somewhat notorious writer, Caradoc Evans. Caradoc's first book, a collection of short stories, *My People,* published in 1915, inflamed the local non-conformist church-folk, but inspired young Dylan and had a profound influence on Dylan's own early *Jarvis Valley* stories.

Dylan was back in Aberystwyth close to the end of his life. In the autumn of 1952 Dylan read to a packed audience in the great Examination Hall of Aberystwyth University with the less fortunate students hovering outside in the indoor quadrangle. Dylan read his own choice of poems by Yeats, Gogarty, Edith Sitwell, Henry Read, Auden, Eliot and Vernon Watkins, before reading some of his own poems. Aneurin Davies, who has written on Dylan as an actor, was one of the lucky students to attend the reading and remembers it clearly:

> The audience was enthralled by the performance that enfolded before it… Dylan read throughout to the accompaniment of nature, for as always in the background was the sound of the sea swirling around what was left of the pier and breaking against the rocks below the promenade.

How fitting for someone named 38 years earlier after the Mabinogion's *Dylan Son of Wave.* The *Cambrian News* also reported on the event:

> It was an unusual evening. Mr Thomas's presence and his dithyrambic way of speaking combined to move his listeners, as it were, out of themselves and induced genuine admiration mingled with involuntary astonishment.

Dylan made many visits and retreats to Cardiganshire, mainly during the war years, to escape the horrors of the Blitz in London – to Talsarn in the summer of 1942 to stay with friends at the small mansion, Gelli, and then to New Quay to live in Majoda in 1944/5. Today these areas are now known, reluctantly by many Welsh folk, as Ceredigion. Talsarn is situated on the river Aeron, which is the source of the name Dylan and Caitlin gave their daughter – Aeronwy (the parents propagated the juicy factoid that

Aeronwy was conceived during an "al fresco" frolic on the banks of the river). In the same ribald way Dylan chooses to share a curious image when writing to his drinking pal Tommy Earp in 1942:

I tossed off this morning over Talsarn Bridge to the fishes.

Dylan also refers in his works to other West Wales towns – Pembroke features as the home of a scissor-wielding, vampire devil, in his early short story, "The School for Witches" (1936). And Pembroke is also the home of the amorous chimney sweep in the ribald and smutty pub song "Come and Sweep My Chimbley", sung with great gusto by Mr Waldo in one of the climactic scenes in *Under Milk Wood*:

I wept through Pembroke City
Poor and barefoot in the snow
Till a kind young woman took pity.
Poor little chimbley sweep she said
Black as the ace of spades
O nobody's swept my chimbley
Since my husband went his ways
Come and sweep my chimbley
She sighed to me with a blush
Bring along your chimbley brush!

The county of Pembrokeshire was used as the setting for two of the films based on Dylan's work. Fishguard was chosen as the location for the 1972 film of *Under Milk Wood* and a number of Hollywood stars, including Burton, Taylor and O'Toole, descended on the small town of Fishguard where, led by the late inimitable Ryan Davies, they provided locals with many fine raucous, rowdy, enjoyable musical and memorable pub nights.

In 1992 film crews and Peter O'Toole (and the late great Ray Gravell made his thespian debut in the film!) were back in Pembrokeshire to film *Rebecca's Daughters*, directed by Karl Francis. Dylan wrote the script in 1948, it was not published until 1965, and the timespan of 44 years between writing and filming in 1992 is something of a record. The script is based on the violent tollgate protests that occurred in the area between 1839 and 1843. They were known as the Rebecca Riots because the protesting local farmers and agricultural works disguised themselves by wearing women's clothes. They choose the name Rebecca from the Book of Genesis:

And they blessed Rebekah and said unto her... let thy seed possess the gate of those which hate them.

It was probably this early incidence of cross-dressing and peasant revolt that attracted Dylan to the story.

Within weeks of the end of his life, in October 1953, Dylan was back in West Wales visiting the seaside town of Tenby. He had been invited to address local literary society and in the event they were treated to perhaps, the first ever solo reading, of a near complete *Under Milk Wood*. Dylan Thomas's main Cardiganshire sojourn was in the coastal fishing town of New Quay, where he lived from September 1945 through into the summer of the next year, and where he found yet another "local" that would become a favourite.

The Black Lion

New Quay

Dylan, Caitlin and baby Aeronwy moved to New Quay and into a rented, small, wood and asbestos bungalow named Majoda, in September of 1944. They would spend just under a year there before moving on in July 1945 to yet another rented house in Sussex. Majoda was situated just to the north of the town. The house name was made up from the names of the landlord's children – Dylan suggested in a letter that he would re-name the place "Catllewdylaer"! He even wrote a short poem about his new home to his friend, the art critic and doyen of London's Fitzrovia Tommy Earp, who, as we shall see, was the recipient of a few impromptu verses inspired by the town:

We've got a new house and it's called Majoda:
Cards, on the Welsh-speaking sea.
And we'll stay in this wood-and-asbestos pagoda
Till the blackout's raised on London and me.

Majoda, although being pretty primitive and run-down, was set on a stunning cliff-top location. Dylan was told about the property by his old Swansea friend Vera Phillips who had subsequently married an army officer William Killick (Dylan was their best man at their wedding in London in 1943). Vera lived virtually next door with her young daughter as her husband William was a captain in the Royal Engineers and often away on active service with the SOE.

Dylan's favourite New Quay pub was The Black Lion – and Dylan became good friends with the landlord, known to everybody as Jack Pat. He also bred whippets and made buttermilk – and it could be Jack who Dylan had in mind when in *Under Milk Wood* the drowned sailors are reminiscing from their watery graves. While one dreams of "rum and laverbread" and another pines for "bosoms and robins", the fourth wants only "buttermilk and whippets". *Under Milk Wood* also owes much to Thomas's 1944 radio script *Quite Early One Morning*, in which The Black Lion features as:

> the pink washed pub, the pub that was waiting for Saturday night as an over-jolly girl waits for sailors.

The broadcast embodies characters and imagined locations that anticipate, and are expanded to reappear in *Under Milk Wood* some ten years later. There is no doubt that New Quay is one of many coastal towns and villages that Dylan visited or lived in, which all contribute something to Dylan's imaginary Llareggub.

The pub also appears in Dylan's 1946 radio broadcast "The Crumbs of One Man's Year":

> as I weaved towards the toppling town and the black loud *LION* where the cat, who purred like a fire, looked out of

THE BLACK LION
NEW QUAY

two cinders at the gently swilling retired sea-captains in the snug-as-a-bug back bar.

And it features in a somewhat scatological verse letter sent in 1944 to Tommy Earp, an art critic, hard drinker, and a good friend to Dylan:

It is time for the Black Lion
But there is only Buckley's unfrisky
Mild. Turned again. Worthington. Never whiskey
I sit at the open window, observing
The salty scene and my Playered gob curving
Down to the wild, umbrella'd and french-lettered
Beach, hearing rise slimy from the Welsh lechered
Caves the cries of the parchs and their flocks . I
Hear their laughter sly as gonococci.

And he goes on to celebrate an impending visit from Augustus John:

On Saturday Augustus comes, bearded
Like Cardy's bard, and howling as Lear did.
A short stay only but how nice. No
One more welcome than the oaktrunked maestro-
No-one but you who'll never come.

Majoda had magnificent sea views and inspired Thomas to produce some of his most memorable work; apart from the radio script *Quite Early One Morning*, he produced some of his most acclaimed poems such as *The Conversation of Prayers, A Refusal to Mourn the Death of a Child...* and the poem addressed to his son Llewelyn, *This Side of the Truth.*

However Dylan found the circumstances in the tiny bungalow not always conducive to creative writing, what with his Caitlin and Vera gabbling and his own and Vera's baby squawking. He writes of Majoda as being his:

shack at the edge of the cliff where my children hop like fleas in a box.

He describes his situation woefully in a letter:

The rooms are tiny, the wall bumpaper-thin, and a friend arrived with another baby with a voice like Caruso's. Now however, I have taken a room in a nearby house: a very quiet house where I can work till I bleed.

The escape room he writes of was an apple store in the gardens of a nearby small mansion, Plas Llanina, which was owned by the wealthy and somewhat eccentric aristocrat Lord Howard de Walden, whose main home was Chirk Castle in north Wales. His grandson described him thus:

An Englishman turned Welshman; he was polymath, poet playwright, soldier artist, Olympic sportsman, medievalist and pioneer.

De Walden helped Dylan out financially as well as allowing him to write in his garden room and in 1944 Dylan inscribed a copy of his recent poetry pamphlet *New Poems* (1943) to his new patron. Howard de Walden may well have had an earlier, and even more significant, influence on Dylan's life. As a keen

This Side Of The Truth.
(for Llewelyn).

This side of the truth,
You may not see, my son,
King of your blue eyes
In the blinding country of youth,
That all is undone,
Under the unminding skies,
Of innocence and guilt
Before you move to make
One gesture of the heart or head,
Is gathered and spilt
Into the winding dark
Like the dust of the dead.

Good and bad, two ways
Of moving about your death
By the grinding sea,
King of your heart in the blind days,
Blow away like breath,
Go crying through you and me
And the souls of all men
Into the innocent
Dark, and the guilty dark, and good
Death, and bad death, and then
In the last element
Fly like the stars' blood,

Like the sun's tears,
Like the moon's seed, rubbish
And fire, the flying rank
Of the sky, King of your six years.
And the wicked wish
Down the beginning of plants
And animals and birds,
Water and light, the earth and sky,
Is cast before you move,
And all your deeds and words,
Each truth, each lie,
Die in unjudging love.

Dylan's original copy of his poem for his son. On the back is a printed notice "Writing Paper is Precious: Please Do Not Waste It"

champion of the theatre and opera he wrote plays and librettos under the pseudonym T E Ellis. We have to go back to October 27th, 1914, when D J Thomas's first and only son was born and he needed a name. The proud father cast around his library looking for inspiration and hit upon "Dylan", at that time a very unusual and uncommon first name.

It is widely held to be taken from *The Mabinogion*, a series of early texts encapsulating the great mythical prose dramas of the Welsh language. D J Thomas, Dylan's father, would have known it in the original Welsh and in Lady Charlotte Guest's translation which was first published in the 1840s but often reprinted. However more recent Thomas biographers and commentators have cited an operatic trilogy *The Cauldron of Annwn*, composed by Joseph Holbrooke, as another likely source, in particular one section, *Dylan, Son of Wave*. The libretto was written by Howard de Walden. Holbrooke's biographer, Michael Freeman cites the press notices of performance of this opera in 1914 – the year of Dylan's birth, as a more likely source for his father's choice of the name for his son. So perhaps this eccentric aristocrat had a hand in naming a great Welsh poet and by default, he influenced a great American singer-songwriter, one Robert Zimmerman, who chose to change his name to Bob Dylan in homage to one of his favourite poets.

In an unpublished letter written in March 1945 from Dylan to Augustus John, The Black Lion gets honourable mentions, mainly on account of the verbal dexterity of one of Dylan's other bohemian friends Mary Keene, who was staying at Majoda. Dylan tells Augustus that:

Mary Keene is at The Black Lion, baffling a good many by her frequent use of a certain one-syllable word and her disinclination to agree with anything spoken by anyone – from remarks about the weather to the price of pigs.

And in the same letter he returns to this theme when he tells Augustus about the impending visit of another great painter and Mary's lover, Matthew Smith:

> I've no idea how long Mary's staying: she is trying to persuade Matthew to come down, but doubts if the Lion would suit him; she herself grumbles at it a lot but seems to like it anyway; and the Lion-er, for their part, have grown used to that small, wicked word on the lips of a woman.

Mary did stay long enough to get embroiled in one of the truly sensational incidents in Dylan's life – it happened the very next day after he wrote the letter to Augustus and it seems to have begun and carried on in The Black Lion. In the quiet of the Apple House in the grounds of Plas Llanina, Dylan worked away enjoying a very productive period, working as he says in a letter, "till I bleed". However one night this creative spell was dramatically interrupted by a burst of machine gun fire.

Captain William Killick had returned home from a mission behind enemy lines in Greece. He was stressed, strained and fatigued, and not well pleased with his wife's close friendship with her bohemian, non-serving, proto-hippie neighbours. He may well have been jealous, perhaps suspecting a cosy *ménage à trois*, and he must have felt totally excluded from their world.

It all came to a head on the night of March 6th. During the day Dylan was meeting with two London film colleagues, John Eldrige and Fanya Fisher, who were staying at The Black Lion. Dylan and his London colleagues went to a few pubs and in The Commercial Inn they encountered Killick. A rather unpleasant and hostile exchange of views on the war occurred, in which Killick verbally attacked Dylan and his friends, but it ended at that.

However they encountered each other again later in the evening in The Black Lion when all parties had drunk more and they clashed again, this time resulting in a nasty physical exchange. Fanya Fisher was a Jew and she and Dylan perceived an element of anti-Semitism in Killick's behaviour. Killick slapped Miss Fisher, she scratched his face, Dylan piled in and a fight ensued. It was quickly broken up and Dylan and his party went back to Majoda. Killick, however, was not finished. He went home, armed himself with his service weapons, including a machine gun and grenade, and proceeded to attack Majoda.

It resulted in Killick being tried for attempted murder. Here is Dylan's courtroom account of the incident:

> a noise came from the back of the house of glass being smashed and the rattle of a machine gun. Bullets were heard flying through the living room, we crouched down as near to the floor as possible… Then Killick came in with the gun… he fired the machine gun into the ceiling and said, "You are nothing but a load of egoists."

Killick was acquitted, his exemplary military

record was cited, as was his state of mind after his dangerous mission. The case was reported in local papers and in the *News of the World*. Dylan was not keen to go to court, and was not in any way vindictive towards Killick, (something that is distorted, and does not come across in the film based on the incident, *The Edge of Love*). The whole incident shook Dylan up quite considerably and he wrote to Vernon Watkins that since it happened, "Caitlin and I go to bed under the bed". The Swansea Dylan Thomas Centre Collection has two interesting original letters about the incident by William Killick himself and some of the contemporary newspaper accounts of the event, and author David N Thomas has recently published two books about Dylan in Cardiganshire with a detailed account of the nasty fracas which could so easily have had a very different and tragic outcome. The "Majoda incident" was recently used as the lynchpin in a major film about Dylan and Caitlin's life during the war years – *The Edge of Love*, directed by John Mayberry and staring Keira Knightley, Sienna Miller and Matthew Rhys. Interestingly, the producer was Rebecca Gilbertson, who is the granddaughter of William Killick. The *Guardian* film blog sums it up:

The *Edge of Love* is too soft on William Killick, too hard on Dylan Thomas.

But the "Majoda incident" aside, Dylan, for the most part, enjoyed his time in New Quay and the wistful ending of *Quite Early One Morning* encapsulates his feelings:

Thus some of the voices of a cliff-perched town at the far end of Wales moved out of sleep and darkness into the newborn, ancient, and ageless morning, moved and were lost.

The Black Lion today

The Black Lion has just re-opened after a major refurbishment and now offers a fine traditional bar with a range of local and draught beers, a restaurant offering good quality and good value food, prepared fresh, on the premises and using locally sourced produce: top quality Welsh Black and rib-eye steaks come from a local Llanon farm and an ever changing specials board features fresh local caught fish when available. The Lion now boasts nine spacious en suite rooms with five having fantastic sea views; but Dylan Thomas remains ubiquitous in the decor which is based on the pub's collection of Dylan Thomas memorabilia.

London

LONDON

"The Capital Punishment"

DYLAN THOMAS was always going to be drawn to London; he felt that it was where he had to be if he was to have any real success as a published poet and writer. In his radio drama *Return Journey* he writes of how he and his pals were going to:

> ring the bells of London and paint it like a tart.

He made his first visit to the city in 1933 to meet fellow poet Pamela Hansford Johnson, the literary pen-friend he had corresponded with after meeting via the poetry pages of the *Sunday Referee*. Pamela later recalled that when she opened the door to him and beheld him for the first time ever, he blurted out, "Have you seen the Gauguins?"

There was a Gauguin exhibition on in London at the time. Dylan would later admit that he had rehearsed this opening gambit all the way on the train from Swansea to Paddington, such was his desire to impress her with his "arty-ness"! After this meeting their relationship developed, and Pamela became his first serious girlfriend – and very nearly his wife.

He spent most of his time, when not with Pamela, staying with his older sister Nancy on her houseboat in Chertsey. In 1934 he returned to stay with Pamela and her family in Battersea and later that year he made a real attempt to leave Swansea and settle in London at 5 Redcliffe Street, on the seedier fringes of Chelsea. He writes to Pamela:

> Janes and I will be coming up… by car fortunately, bearing with us typewriters, easels, bedclothes, brassieres for lady models, and plum cakes for Nelson's lions – a cherry or two for Eros.

The Redcliffe "flat" was a sordid single room, which he shared with Alfred Janes and Mervyn Levy, two Swansea artists studying at London art schools and both stalwart members of Swansea's Kardomah gang. The landlady had the splendid name of Mrs Parsnip and the place stank of them and other over-cooked vegetables. Undaunted, Dylan immediately sent a very proud and ebullient postcard to another of his Swansea pals, Daniel Jones, who was in lodgings in Harrow. Dylan christened himself and his flatmates as "the mannered pigs".

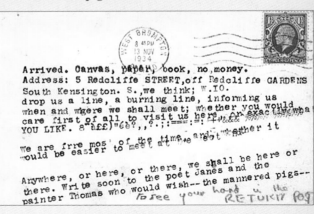

He quickly settled in and was soon writing back to Swansea to his friend Bert Trick that he was wallowing in a:

> muddled and messy room and surrounded by… nothing but poems poems poems butter eggs and mashed potatoes among stories and Janes' canvases… in the quarter of the pseudo-artists, of beards… haughty expressions… and the most boring Bohemian parties I have ever thought possible.

Dylan managed only a few months before he was back in Swansea for some home comforts. However with more and more of his poems being published in a plethora of London-based literary periodicals, he became a frequent visitor, often staying with one or other of his new literary friends. When, in 1936, he met Caitlin Macnamara in The Wheatsheaf pub this pattern of being in and out of London became the model for the rest of his life. He and Caitlin rented a succession of awful flats in Chelsea and Camden. Later the Blitz would send them scurrying back to some safer country bolthole in Wales, or wherever they could find a cheap, or preferably free, place to stay.

As with many of the places he lived, Dylan would oscillate between liking and loathing them, depending on how things were going. Initially he wrote Pamela Hansford Johnson that he was looking for:

> a high conventional garret, there to invoke the sadistic Muses, and get a little drunk on air.

After his first short burst of the full London experience, he was back in Cornwall with friends, recuperating from an overdose of:

Caitlin and Aeronwy at the unveiling of the blue plaque on the flat they rented with Dylan for a brief time in Delancy Street in Camden in the 1950s

promiscuity, booze, coloured shirts, too much talk, too little work.

So it would continue. For various reasons he could not keep away from the city, but he begins to refer to it as "nightmare London", and he complains:

> even the sun's grey and God how I hate it.

Writing to Vernon Watkins in 1938 Dylan tells him:

> I've just come back from three dark days in London, city of the restless dead. It really is an insane city, & filled me with terror.

Dylan takes the sun on a London rooftop – snapped by Mervyn Levy

And by 1941 he is having real difficulties:

We arrived with no money… In Laugharne that was not so bad. In stinking friendless London it is unendurable.

When he writes in his unfinished novel *Adventures in the Skin Trade* (1955) of London being a city:

of knickerless women, enamouring from cane tables, waiting in the fumes for the country cousins to stagger in, all savings and haywisps.

he seems to be describing the experiences of a country boy like himself.

LONDON

The Fitzroy Tavern

Charlotte Street

"If you haven't visited The Fitzroy, you haven't visited London" – Augustus John

THE GREAT BOHEMIAN PAINTER Augustus John begins his memoir of his friend Dylan Thomas:

I met Dylan first at The Fitzroy Tavern, Charlotte Street. William Empsom was also present so the meeting was doubly memorable.

He ends it:

With his departure, the tavern has lost its finest ornament and henceforth I, for one, intend to drink at home, but to Dylan's memory all the same.

The Fitzroy Tavern is situated on the corner of Charlotte Street and Windmill Street, in the area of London to which it lends its name. The area is roughly bounded by Euston Road in the North, Oxford Street in the South, Gower Street to the East and Great Portland Street to the west. Historically it was always an area which attracted artists and writers from the

THE FITZROY TAVERN.

WlynThomas
2012

eighteenth century onwards. The sculptor Nollekens, and Blake's friend, the artist Fuseli, lived there, and they were followed by Richard Wilson, Constable, Landseer, Rossetti and Walter Sickert. It was also the sometime home to Thomas Paine and Edmund Burke, and later Karl Marx attended political meetings in Charlotte Street and Rathbone Place. George Bernard Shaw lived in Fitzroy Square, as did Virginia Woolf. She lived on the square between 1907 and 1911, but she is more closely linked to the neighbouring area of Bloomsbury, which the Fitzrovians regarded as affected and effete. The decadent French poet Arthur Rimbaud lived with his partner Paul Verlaine in Howland Street. Rimbaud was to become a kind of hero for young Dylan Thomas, who would proudly describe himself as:

> Good old 3-adjectives-a-penny, belly-churning Thomas, the Rimbaud of Cwmdonkin Drive.

The term Fitzrovia was first used during the interwar years by the louche habitués of the area, but then it became more widely used in recognition of how this bohemian community of artists, writers, composers and entertainers had made its pubs, drinking clubs and restaurants their own. The name is generally credited to have been first used in print by the colourful left-wing politician and journalist, Tom Driberg MP, when writing in his pseudonymous *Daily Express* William Hickey column in 1940.

The pub is named either directly or indirectly after the Fitzroy family, the Dukes of Grafton, who owned much of the land on which Fitzrovia came to be built.

The building was originally constructed in 1883 as the Fitzroy Coffee House, but converted to a pub (called "The Hundred Marks") in 1887, by William Mortimer Brutton. In the early years of the twentieth century, Judah Morris Kleinfeld purchased it, and he rebranded it The Fitzroy Tavern in March 1919.

Kleinfeld was a Russian Jewish refugee, a huge, man-mountain of a fellow who had been a tailor, but it was as a pub landlord he made his mark. He

Self-portrait by Augustus John drawn in the Fitzroy

was ably assisted by his daughter Annie, who helped behind the bar and did all the book-keeping, as Judah could not write English. It was "Pop" Kleinfeld's larger-than-life personality which attracted writers, artists and composers to what became the foremost bohemian pub in the area. The pub was closed on Rosh Hashanah and Yom Kippur. Judah Kleinfeld retired from the pub in the fifties and it was taken on by Annie and her husband Charlie Allchild. Their daughter Sally Fiber was born in the pub, worked behind the bar from a young age and eventually wrote a lively history, *The Fitzroy: The Autobiography of a London Tavern* (1995).

The Fitzroy bar consisted of an L-shaped saloon bar and a smaller public bar, which came complete with a sawdust strewn floor, an electric pianola, and a bar stocked with a dubious collection of curious potent bottles, which included a pepper-based concoction known as a Jerusalem Brandy. The pub's interior design motif was "patriotism and the forces". The walls were covered with an array of mainly First World War militaria: cap badges, helmets, flags, insignia and ancient jingoistic recruiting posters.

The ceiling looked like it was suffering from a disgusting fungal condition but closer inspection revealed that the bumpy irregular protuberances were bundles of scrunched paper money or twists of small change fixed to the ceiling with darts. This was a custom instigated by Pop Kleinfeld, who would periodically take down this bounty, pile it on the bar, and with great ceremony, and sometimes with a celebrity helper, count it up. The money, often a quite remarkable sum, was used to fund parties and

How to find The Fitzroy Tavern in the Blackout: a wartime notice on the wall of the pub

outings for local children and it became known as the *Pennies from Heaven* charity.

The liveliest period for Fitzrovia was between the mid-20s and the years just after the end of the Second World War.

Many of the characters who enlivened the pub then are now consigned to the byways of literary history. Art critic Tommy Earp, the Scottish poet and writer Ruthven Todd and the Australian brothers Jack and Philip Lindsay, are not widely known now, but back then they were ubiquitous, and they were all to become close friends of Dylan Thomas.

It was a Swansea friend who introduced Dylan to the pub. Trevor Hughes, Dylan's companion in his story "Who Do You Wish Was With Us", had left Swansea to work as a clerk in London, but he also had literary inclinations. He and Dylan shared a rich correspondence and friendship and Trevor recollects:

> I introduced him to The Fitzroy Tavern... The first time he came to London... he'd heard so much about these bohemian pubs in the West End. Did I know of any typically bohemian pub where I could take him? I thought immediately of The Fitzroy. I was not a drinking man at all in those days but I had come up to London to work; I was staying in Bloomsbury at the time.

This was in 1933, and Dylan was eager to make a return visit to stay with Trevor at Raynes Park and in January 1934 he is writing to Trevor looking forward to visiting him when:

> if nothing else we can spend a few hours together in The Fitzroy Tavern.

These first few visits to The Fitzroy are described in detail by Trevor in the course of an interview recorded by Colin Edwards. Hughes reveals some interesting things about Dylan in this pub, at this time. What comes over most, is that this is Dylan before any real literary success or fame. He is in The Fitzroy as a regular everyday punter, and he and Trevor enjoy the lively atmosphere, but also are very content in their own company:

> He liked the social atmosphere, and I do know that, so far as he and I were concerned, we could sit in The Fitzroy Tavern on a Saturday night – it would be absolutely full of people. Somebody playing the piano in the old tinky-tonky way… Tremendous hub-bub all about us. And in that atmosphere, Dylan and I could be more alone and less self-conscious than we would be anywhere else. And in that environment, we could discuss things without embarrassment… and Dylan did not want to drink – no, he wanted to talk.

This seems to change as Dylan became a more well-known and recognisable literary figure. By the time Dylan arrived in London in 1934, he had already had a number of poems and a few reviews published in significant London literary magazines such as *The Adelphi* and T S Eliot's *Criterion*. His reputation was slowly growing among editors and other writers. In 1934 the current crop of Fitzrovians was dominated by two artists, Augustus John and Nina Hamnett, who were both from the South West Wales seaside town of Tenby. They were born at either end of the same seafront street but did not meet until they got to London. On this meeting, in The Fitzroy, Augustus declared to Nina that:

> we are the sort of people our fathers warned us against.

Augustus John loved The Fitzroy – he likened it to "Clapham Junction – sooner or later everyone has to pass through it", and of the landlord he declared:

> If I knew the yiddisher for "gentleman" I would use it to define Mr Kleinfeld.

Artists were thick on the ground – Percy Wyndham Lewis, Michael Ayrton, John Minton, and the two Scots Roberts, Coloquhoun and MacBryde. They were joined by writers and literary figures such as George Orwell, Maclaren-Ross, the Sitwells and the handsome Sri Lankan, Meary Tambimuttu, known just as Tambi. To these can be added the assorted, hard to pigeon-hole, characters such as "The Great Beast" Aleister Crowley, showgirl and model Betty May – known as The Tiger Lady, Albert Pierrepoint, the long serving "official" hangman, and the colourful African racing tipster Crown Prince Monolulu, whose dress code consisted of garish silk jackets, one of which was decorated with "good luck" talismanic designs mixing four-leafed clovers, horseshoes and winning posts, and this outfit would be topped off with a feather plumed native headdress. No wonder heads turned when he entered the pub bellowing out his catchphrase, "I gotta horse!"

The artist Nina Hamnett, the Queen of Bohemia to Augustus John's King, was part of the furniture of The Fitzroy Tavern. Dylan's friend and first biographer, Constantine Fitzgibbon, wrote:

> To enter Kleinfeld's and not buy Nina a drink, was in those days and in that world, a solecism that amounted to a social stigma.

Her usual first greeting was a blunt, "Hello ducks! Mine's a double gin". Her quid pro quo could be either a spontaneous recitation from her store of bawdy limericks:

> *There was a young girl of Adowa*
> *Whose quim was the shape of a flower*
> *She was so very teeny*
> *It intrigued Mussolini*
> *Who put off the War for an hour.*

Or she would launch into one of her many polished anecdotes about one of her many torrid affairs; her lovers included Roger Fry, Gaudier-Brzeska and Modigliani. She met Picasso and Eric Satie, and "entertained" Diaghilev, Stravinsky, Cocteau and Valentino!

She was never backward in coming forward; when Dylan introduced her to Ruthven Todd in The Fitzroy,

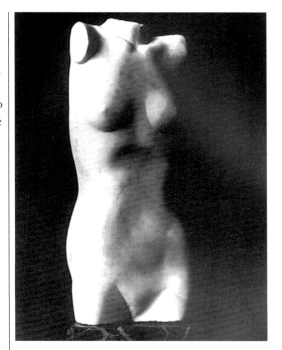

Gaudier-Brzeska's bust – Nina Hamnett was his model

Nina exclaimed loudly for all the pub's denizens to hear:

> You know me, m'dear – I'm in the V and A with me left tit knocked off!

She was referring to the marble torso that one of her many lovers, Henri Gaudier-Brzeska, had made of her which then went on display in the V & A but has since moved to the Tate. It also provided the title for her celebrated biography *Laughing Torso* (1932). She was inordinately proud of her chest, and with a tad too much gin in her was prone to boast to anyone that Modigliani said she had:

The best tits in Europe

and then she shocked her audience by hoisting up her tatty old jersey and showing them off! By a curious synchronicity *Laughing Torso* was responsible for ending Dylan Thomas's none-too-promising career as a local journalist. In 1933 Dylan had published an article in the *South Wales Evening Post* entitled "Genius and Madness Akin in World of Art". It is an interesting piece, but in it, he made a rather careless and inaccurate reference to Nina (who at that time he had never met), describing her as "the author of the banned book *Laughing Torso*". The next week the paper carried a formal and fulsome apology for the error and it concluded:

We are informed by Miss Hamnett that *Laughing Torso* enjoys a very wide circulation.

Almost immediately Dylan's employment at the *Post* was terminated but later Dylan, with characteristic hyperbole, boasts about this in his further efforts to impress Pamela Hansford Johnson:

I ran the Northcliffe Press into a libel suit by calling Miss Hamnett insane. Apparently she wasn't, that was the trouble.

Dylan's friend Desmond Hawkins recalls being in The Fitzroy with Dylan when:

Nina joined us and asked if he had read her autobiography. "Read it?" he replied. "I certainly have. Had to review it for a Welsh newspaper and the editor was sued for it, so I was sacked."

Nina lived a rich and colourful life but the drink eventually got to her and she became a sad figure, and in 1956 she died after falling from the balcony of her flat and impaling herself on the spiked railing below. The London Welsh writer Rhys Davies contributed a warm memoir of her to Keidrych Rhys's revamped *Wales* magazine, in which he recalls:

as I sat waiting for her coffin to be borne in she would not have minded… that I remembered her telling me, "I took my grey dress to the dry cleaners and, my dear, it just shrivelled up because of all the gin soaked into it over the years. All they gave me back was a spoonful of dust."

When John Malcolm Brinnin arrived in London in 1951 he made the mistake of revealing to Dylan that

it was around his birthday. Dylan and Nina Hamnett decided a Fitzrovian binge was called for and during the course of the long night Dylan and Nina both inscribed and embellished a battered copy of Dylan's *Deaths and Entrances* as a memento for their weary American friend; Dylan drew a detailed bar room scene and Nina added a spirited sketch of a topless dancer!

Dylan thought enough of Nina to write her affectionately into the *roman à clef* he wrote with John Davenport, *The Death of the King's Canary* (published posthumously in 1978). In it Nina appears as:

> Yvonne Bacon, pillar of Charlotte Street, monument of the old Dome, collector of celebrities, professional introducer.

Litigation of one sort or another seems to be a loose thread that ties some of The Fitzroy's characters together. Nina, who went after young Dylan over his article mentioning *Laughing Torso,* was later sued by Aleister Crowley for what she wrote about him in the same book!

The Fitzrovians were a broad church, and prided themselves on their liberal, live-and-let-live attitudes, but even they were unsure about Aleister Crowley. Dylan knew of him as a curiosity but not really as a friend. In fact Dylan seemed to be afraid of him which is hardly surprising given his depiction in the popular press – the popular magazine *John Bull*, described him bluntly as "A Man We'd Like to Hang" (perhaps the hangman Albert Pierpoint, another Fitzroy regular, could have obliged!). Crowley would later appear up above and to the left of Dylan Thomas on the seminal record album design by Peter Blake for the Beatles' Sgt Pepper LP.

Crowley was known by a number of strange names – "Frater Perdurabo", "666", "Baphomet", or more often, the self-styled "Great Beast". He was a truly bizarre man.

Crowley was also linked to Dylan via Victor Neuberg, a middle-aged bisexual, who was to become Dylan's literary godfather. In the early thirties Neuberg was a literary journalist, and was appointed editor of the Poet's Corner feature in the *Sunday Referee*, which was trying to grow its circulation as a middle ground, popular Sunday newspaper. Neuberg was immediately taken by the poems sent in by a young Welshman, and in September, 1933, Neuberg published Dylan's poem *That Sanity be Kept*. Neuberg added his own personal evaluation of the poem declaring it:

> perhaps the best modernist poem that as yet I've received; its psychology is exquisite.

POEM.

The silken sky that draws my dreams
Displays a bribery of stars
That I can rattle in my hand:
The moon is lurking in the limes,
And in her darkened doorway, bears
A rushlight for the journeyman.

All night the knowledgeable trees,
With honey-dropping fingers, strew
The firmament with slender scents:
The flowers flicker, and their eyes
Upon my silver body prey
Too coldly for their innocence.

The earth desires me, and my mouth,
Tormented by my own desire,
Is drier than a summer grave:
The grasses tremble at my breath,
And I, Prometheus shorn of fire,
Am surfeited with seedless love.

P. MELA HANSFORD JOHNSON.

POEM.

Foster the light, nor veil the feeling moon,
Nor sister globes that fall not on the bone,
But strip and bless the marrow in the
    spheres;
Master the night, nor spite your starry
    spine,
Nor muster worlds that course not through
    the skin,
But know the clays that burrow round the
    stars.

Murmur of spring, nor crush the roaring
    eggs,
Nor hammer back the season in the figs,
But wind the summer-bearer in your get;
Farmer the wilds, nor fill the corny bogs,
Nor harm a weed that wars not in your legs,
But set and grow a meadow in the heart.

Move you unmarrowed in your ragged shifts,
O sea and sky, nor sorrow as this flesh
Goes from another with a nitric smile;
Nor as my bones are bridled on her shafts,
Nor when my locks are shooting in the turf,
Shall grief go salty-lidded in the gales.

One gave the clouds their colours and their
    shapes;
One gave me clay, and dyed the crowded sea
with the green wings of fish and flying men.
Set you your waves and daylights on my
    lips,
Give me your tempers and your tides as I
Have grafted flesh on to the sea and sun.

DYLAN THOMAS.

Poet's Corner from an October 1934 edition of the Sunday Referee. *Dylan's poem is below that of his girlfriend Pamela Hansford Johnson*

Neuberg continued to publish Dylan's early poems in his column – including *The Force that Through the Green Fuse Drives the Flower*, and in April 1934 he announced that Dylan Thomas had been awarded the paper's Book Prize, which meant that the *Sunday Referee* would sponsor the immediate publication of the winning poet's first book; Pamela Hansford Johnson had been a previous winner. Publication was slow, but late in 1934, a small edition of just 250 copies of *18 Poems* was published in an elegant and minimalist edition, designed and printed by the Favil Press. Dylan was forever greatly indebted to "The Vicky-bird", his affectionate name for Neuberg.

18
POEMS

DYLAN THOMAS

Published by
THE SUNDAY REFEREE and
THE PARTON BOOKSHOP
PARTON STREET. LONDON. W.C.1

The elegant title-page of Dylan Thomas's rare first book

However, some thirty years earlier Neuberg was not a "Vicky bird" but a "Vicky camel"!

Around 1906, the 26-year-old Neuberg was an undergraduate in Cambridge where he was drawn into Aleister Crowley's magical web. Neuberg was already a published poet, and Crowley had been attracted by the mystical leanings in his poems. Crowley, affluent, charming, and urbane, was himself an erudite fellow poet, although his book of erotic poems *White Stains* (1898), which he had printed in a small edition, was in large part seized by UK customs, who destroyed most of the copies. Crowley began to exert a magnetic and sexually charged grip over Neuberg, who quickly became one of his acolytes, and was duly received into his magical Order, the AA, and given the magical name of "Frater Omnia Vincam".

Thus began Crowley's long-lasting sentimental relationship with Neuberg. In 1909, Crowley took Neuberg to Algiers, and they set off into the North African desert, where they performed a series of occult rituals based on the Enochian system of Doctor John Dee, the early Welsh scientist and alchemist, who was regarded as the Queen's Sorcerer in the court of Elizabeth I. (He is thought to be Shakespeare's model for Prospero in *The Tempest*.) These events were later chronicled in Crowley's book *The Vision and the Voice*. It transpired that in the midst of these bizarre escapades, Crowley first introduced his ideas of sex and magic together and began performing his "sex magick" rituals with the besotted Neuberg. Shortly thereafter Neuberg and Crowley had a violent quarrel; Crowley is said to have put a heavy curse on Neuberg which became the source of the apocryphal tale that Crowley had turned Neuburg into a camel and he was incarcerated in Cairo Zoo!

Neuburg had tried to put all these events well behind him by the time he was publishing young Dylan's work, and although Dylan would sometimes ridicule Neuburg about his extraordinary past, when Neuburg died in 1947, Dylan wrote this warm tribute to him:

> He possessed I believe many kinds of genius, and not the least was his genius for drawing to himself, by his wisdom, graveness, great humour and innocence, a feeling of trust and love that won't ever be forgotten.

Yet another notable Fitzroy character to be dragged into this curious web was Betty May – aka The Tiger Woman. Betty May was born and raised in the slums of the East End, where she endured an extremely rough childhood. But she blossomed against the odds into a beautiful young woman; she was taken up as an artist's model, and this led her into decidedly bohemian circles. She migrated to Paris where she hung out with a gang of motorised robbers known as The Apaches, where her ferocity in gang fights earned her her nickname. But she was very upwardly mobile and was married three times: her second husband divorced her because of her overuse of cocaine; having cleaned up she married again for love.

She met her third husband, the exotically named Raoul Loveday, at Harlequin Club in London. He was a young Oxford graduate and keen Egyptologist. This interest brought the couple into Crowley's sphere and in 1923 The Great Beast took them off on a fateful visit to his infamous retreat, Thelema Abbey in Cefalù, on the Island of Sicily. There a series of bizarre events led to the death of Loveday. Betty May held Crowley responsible but he was never charged. On her return to England she sold her story in all its proto-tabloid gory details to the *Sunday Express*, which included her story in its ongoing attacks on Crowley. With these and similar rumours about activities at the Abbey in mind, Benito Mussolini's government demanded that Crowley leave the country.

Crowley would later sue Nina Hamnett for revelations relating to him and his sex magic practices at Thelema which she included in *Laughing Torso*. Nina called Betty May as her star witness. Although Betty was given quite a rough ride by Crowley's barrister – she was forced to admit that the Apache story was somewhat short on truth – the popular press had a field day. In the end Justice Swift threw Crowley's case out and declared that he had:

> never heard such dreadful and horrible, blasphemous and abominable stuff.

Nina was again vindicated and Crowley was declared bankrupt.

To look at, Betty May was a petite and angelic woman, but she had ferocious green eyes, which matched her fiery temperament. The writer Arthur Calder Marshall recalls seeing her leaving a seedy hotel in Fitzrovia followed by five men; "she was conspicuously dressed in a coat of tiger-skin with a cap to match". Dylan was drawn to her, maybe because one of his bar-room antics was to crawl around the pub on

Betty May – The Tiger Woman

all fours like a dog, nipping the ankles of unsuspecting drinkers. Betty May's party trick was to squat down on all fours and lap up drink from a saucer like her eponymous jungle feline. Despite her being a good bit older than Dylan, he seemed inclined towards playing "cats and dogs" with her. He admits these amorous designs towards her in a letter to Bert Trick:

> I have met a number of new notabilities including Henry Moore, Edwin and Willa Muir, Wyndham Lewis and certainly not least Betty May... Betty May is, as you probably know, an artist's model who has posed – perhaps that is not the correct word – for John, Epstein and the rest

of the racketeers. She wrote a book to describing herself as "The Tiger Woman of Paris"... I am going to write an article for her, under her name, for the *News of the World*. My payment will not be monetary, but, and although she is now not as young as she was, that will not matter.

Dylan's death in 1953 drew people who had known him back to The Fitzroy. Trevor Hughes who had first introduced Dylan to the pub spoke of how:

> at the news of his illness I went back to the Fitzroy Tavern where I felt, I might get near to him. I had some irrational idea that contemplating, not the death of a drunk, but the moving of a great man into the mystic night, and that I, helpless, could only love, and question not, and seek to uphold, even after death.

Sally Fiber describes a night in November 1953, when Wynford Vaughan Thomas came into the bar looking very distressed. He told Annie that he had just heard of the terrible news of Dylan's death. Annie remembered the days she had thrown him out of The Fitzroy... but she readily agreed to Wynford's strange request,

> Would you allow me to hold a memorial service to Dylan in the bar tonight?

That evening a most moving short service took place in the saloon bar of The Fitzroy conducted by Wynford in honour of his friend. At the end Wynford passed his hat around and the donations were then thrown on the ceiling so that Dylan's memory provided a day's fun for local kids.

The Fitzroy today

As late as 1968 Pamela Hansford Johnson included a "Dylan-like character" in her novel *The Survival of the Fittest* and she has him inveigle a rich patron to pay for a trip to The Fitzroy! Today, the vast collection of framed photos on the walls, depicting the pub's past and its former denizens are testament to the pub's claims to be the greatest literary and showbiz pub in London. Along with Dylan Thomas, the eclectic cast includes the great Tommy Cooper, Albert Pierrepoint, George Orwell, George Bernard Shaw, Richard Attenborough, Walter Sickert, Coco the Clown, and *Goon Show* star Michael Bentine.

The pub today is more of a Fitzrovian tourist curiosity. It is popular with UCL students and *The Cheese Grater,* the alternative UCL student magazine, holds weekly gatherings there. Since the 1980s The Fitzroy Tavern has been a regular gathering place for fans of *Doctor Who*. They meet, informally, on the first Thursday evening of each month. Since 2000 it has been the home of the Pear Shaped Comedy Club which runs every Wednesday in the downstairs bar.

THE WHEATSHEAF

The Wheatsheaf

25 Rathbone Place

THE WHEATSHEAF, in the heart of Fitzrovia, is the pub where, in April 1936, Dylan Thomas first met his wife-to-be, the attractive Irish dancer, and sometime artist's model, Caitlin Macnamara. She was with Augustus John, who was painting her and routinely ravishing her. She apparently did not find this very pleasant but went along with it because, she said, she knew no different. She was born into, and raised by, an Irish bohemian family, the Macnamaras, who hailed from Ennistymon in the West of Ireland, but had moved to Hampshire to be near Augustus John's tribe at Fryern Court. Francis Macnamara, Caitlin's father, was a minor Irish litterateur and poet and a friend of Augustus. Francis believed in and advocated doctrines of free love but the John household took notions of bohemian life to even wilder extremes.

For both Dylan and Caitlin, their meeting in The Wheatsheaf was love at first sight. Caitlin's previous experiences with men led her to believe that "all men were bastards". Yet from the moment she met him she felt Dylan was somehow different. Caitlin comments on how, no sooner had they been introduced, Dylan, with surprising physical elasticity, had managed to get his head onto Caitlin's lap. He then proceeded to stare up at her, cherubic and doe-eyed, drunkenly insisting that she was the most beautiful woman he had ever met and that he was going to marry her; she offered no objections. Later that day, they crept away from the Augustus John drunken posse and booked into the nearby Eiffel Tower Hotel. They slept together that night; Caitlin describing Dylan's love-making as:

nothing sensational …

but adequate enough to keep them at it; sleeping late; days leisurely pub-crawling; then back to their "love nest" hotel for the night. Thus they carried on for five or six nights – apparently without eating! When they eventually left, Caitlin cheekily charged the room to Augustus John who was a regular patron of the establishment's restaurant.

However, as is the case with most of the significant episodes in Dylan's life, all of the above may not be entirely factual. It is drawn largely from the account that Caitlin writes as the opening for her 1986 memoir *Caitlin: Life with Dylan Thomas*. In the most recent biography, Andrew Lycett's *Dylan Thomas* (2004), we are warned that some details of this legendary first meeting may well have been embroidered, for example, that when Thomas slipped out of his trousers later that evening back in the hotel, his trousers were so dirty they stood in the corner by themselves; and he also calls into question their charging the room to Augustus.

Paul Ferris also suggests that the chronology is hard to substantiate in the light of other facts. The surviving accounts of the event by the main participants – Caitlin, Dylan and Augustus John – are all at odds over details and later biographies differ quite significantly. However, details apart, what is true is that they met in The Wheatsheaf, and that, after a few hiccups, some fifteen months later, on July 11th, 1937, Dylan married Caitlin at Penzance Register Office. They were to remain married, albeit somewhat tempestuously, for the sixteen remaining years of Dylan's life.

The writer Rayner Heppenstall, a novelist critic and all round litterateur, was one of Dylan's more awkward London pals. He wrote an interesting memoir *Four Absentees* (1960). The four in question are Dylan, Orwell, Eric Gill and J Middleton Murray. In it he recalls his first meeting with Dylan and Caitlin:

I went into The Wheatsheaf… there I found Dylan Thomas whom I had not seen for a year. With him was his future wife Caitlin. I had not met her before, and my first impression was of how extraordinarily alike the two were.

Shortly after this meeting Rayner and his wife joined Dylan and Caitlin in Cornwall, at the Lobster Pot guest house in Mousehole. They enjoyed "an evening drinking in Lamorna" and "a morning occasion in a sunny field above Newlyn":

Dylan was carrying around with him and intermittently sipping from a flagon of "champagne wine tonic", a Penzance herbalist's highly intoxicating brew sold cheaply

without licence. Dylan talked copiously then stopped. "Somebody's boring me," he said. "I think it's me."

The Wheatsheaf remained a regular call for the couple, and for Dylan when he was in London alone. Writing to Keidrych Rhys in 1936, he informs him:

> I shall be in town Thursday July 30 just for the day, and shall spend licensed hours in The Wheatsheaf.

It was the pub that Dylan and Julian Maclaren-Ross sought kingship of, but without resorting to physical violence. Dan Davin, a New Zealander who worked in publishing in London and Oxford after war service, knew both Dylan and Julian, and in his memoir *Closing Time* (1975), he explains how it worked:

> [Dylan] was a good deal in London and often to be seen or found in The Wheatsheaf... Julian was a conversational monopolist and exacted total attention from his audience – something Dylan, himself always his own centre and never short of listeners... would never be willing to concede... So when Dylan came into The Wheatsheaf, he always turned right at the door; Julian who never seemed to arrive in The Wheatsheaf but always seemed to be already there, kept his station at the corner of the bar on the left.

Davin also recounts an interesting episode in The Wheatsheaf on a Saturday morning. Dylan happened upon Dan and joined him over a pint. Dan told Dylan he was reading Dylan's *Portrait of the Artist as a Young Dog*... and how much he admired the stories, and then questioned Dylan as to why he had parodied James Joyce's title – Joyce's early stories were published as *Portrait of the Artist as a Young Man*:

> his brown eyes bulged at me and then down to his beer, dog-hung. He explained that he hadn't read James Joyce at the time.

Davin was "startled, shocked":

> I could not see how he could have written the stories without reading Joyce.

Long afterwards Davin discovered that his intuition was indeed correct and Dylan had read Joyce, "and carefully". By then Davin had his own theories to explain Dylan's behaviour:

> I already knew from much listening to Dylan that he was from time to time overcome by a strange compulsion to give evasive answers to simple questions, invent unnecessary falsehoods, construct complicated fantasies, as if there were something too boring about simple truth, or as if the muscles of his imagination occasionally insisted on flexing themselves however inappropriate the occasion.

What hope is there for biographers in the face of such mischievous duplicity on Dylan's part?

Opposite: Nora Summers' fine photograph of Dylan and Caitlin – "Just Married"

The Wheatsheaf today

The Wheatsheaf is still a busy thriving pub that serves a wide selection of licensed drinks and traditional British cuisine. They have regular comedy slots on Saturdays. There is also an upstairs wine bar and restaurant. They can cater for private parties of up to 60 people and provide outside seating on the pavement.

Other London pubs

DYLAN DRANK in pubs and clubs all around central London. Here is a brief round-up of some of his favourites.

The Stags Head

A pub near the BBC. Maclaren Ross describes an incident when Dylan's patron and "ardent" (the derogatory word he used to describe his gushing female acolytes), Margaret Taylor, swept into the bar looking for Dylan, who immediately ducked down beneath the flap at the end of the bar. Julian found it hard to keep a straight face as she interrogated him as to the poet's whereabouts while he kept glimpsing Dylan's hand "snaking stealthily up to retrieve his pint".

The French House

Originally called The Wine House when it opened in 1910, the pub was bought in 1914 by a Belgian, Victor

just two: After the fall of France in the Second World War, General Charles de Gaulle escaped to London where he formed the Free French Forces. His speech rallying the French people, *À tous les Français*, is said to have been written in the pub. So one major work was written there, another was almost lost there, for The French is one of the many Soho pubs that claim to be

Berlemont, who had moved to London in 1900, and he changed the name of the pub to The York Minster. He was succeeded by his son Gaston Berlemont, who was born in the pub in 1914, and worked there until his retirement in 1989.

The pub has many claims to fame but herewith

MEARD STREET W1
CITY OF WESTMINSTER

SITE OF MANDRAKE AND GARGOYLE CLUBS.

SHOPPEARE

the pub where Dylan left the manuscript of *Under Milk Wood*. The name was changed to The French House after the fire at York Minster in 1984. Contributions toward the cathedral's restoration fund started arriving at the pub. Upon forwarding them, Gaston Berlemont found that the cathedral had been receiving deliveries of claret intended for him! The pub walls are hung with an amazing collection of fading signed photographs of vanished boxers, old music hall stars and writers of the 1930s.

The Gargoyle Club

An infamous, but sadly now defunct, private drinking club founded by an interesting eccentric, Stephan Tennant who befriended Dylan. Osbert Sitwell left a vivid picture of the couple flouncing into the Gargoyle Club in Soho, where artists mixed with the more louche members of the aristocracy. Sitwell found Thomas "an utterly impossible but quite fascinating person". After an incident somewhere else, where Caitlin had gone berserk and broken the arm of Sitwell's cousin, Virginia Gilliatt, he reported Thomas trying to outperform his wife, as he raced into The Gargoyle one night and spun down the stairs:

> Once on the dancing floor (he was poetically dressed in tweeds, with curls of hair like Bacchus, shoes, but no socks), he ripped off both shoes and danced barefoot… He moved on to the table where David Tennant was sitting drinking a valuable bottle of claret, poured it into his own shoe and drank it, finished the bottle, and then with an extraordinary gliding movement, like a sea serpent, traversed the entire floor to the far end of the room and landed on the divan, nestling his head against the thighs of Harold Nicolson, whom he hates.

The evening ended with the Thomases getting into a fight and having to be ejected. The Gargoyle is now a fine restaurant but they sometimes have music nights upstairs. Nearby was…

The Mandrake Club

A seedier version of The Gargoyle.

> In order to circumnavigate the licensing laws which specified that outside normal pub hours alcohol could only be served with food, customers had to buy a token sandwich – usually a dried-up, well-handled inedible specimen. Whenever a tiro member had the temerity to complain, the scruffy bear-like Bulgarian proprietor Boris would march over to their table and, in the voice of a teacher admonishing a difficult child, explain, "This sandwich is for drinking with, not for eating".
>
> – John Heath Stubbs

Now an Indian restaurant.

The Salisbury

A magnificent Victorian edifice; a riot of etched crystal glass and mahogany; still a proper boozer with sausage and mash and good beer. The great photographer Bill Brandt took some defining images of Dylan Thomas in this pub for a feature "Young Poets of Democracy" published in *Lilliput* magazine in 1941.

America

AMERICA

Searching for naked women in mackintoshes

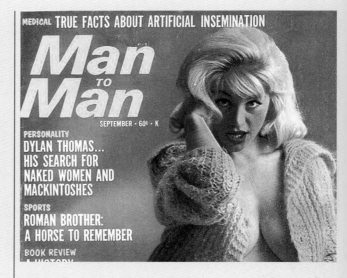

J AMES A DAVIES suggests that Dylan's journey to America was somehow inevitable:

Throughout his life Thomas had unwittingly prepared himself for this encounter with the new world at its extreme.

He cites Dylan's lifelong love of Hollywood films and gangster novels, and elsewhere he cites another motive: Dylan's admiration for Charles Dickens. He suggests that they:

both saw visiting America as the desirable response to uneasy lives and the lack of financial security, both gave themselves to a demanding public, and both were destroyed by the whole affair... In other crucial ways his tours were like his predecessor's... "I'll go to America," says the troubled young man in what is arguably Dickens's greatest comic novel. In 1950 Dylan Thomas was Martin Chuzzlewit redivivus.

Dylan's work had begun to appear in American magazines early on but his first American publication was *The World I Breathe*, a collection of poetry and prose which came out in 1939, published by James Laughlin's *New Directions*. They would publish most of his work in America but it was often packaged in a different way and his great poem *Do Not Go Gentle Into That Good Night* was first published in an American book *In Country Sleep* (1952) some six months before the poem was published in the UK. Dylan described his visits to America to Princess Caetani, his rich Italian patron and the editor of *Botteghe Oscure*:

I buried my head in the sands of America: flew over America like a damp, ranting bird; boomed and fiddled while home was burning.

Dylan facetiously alludes to these tensions. In the States he found "appreciation, dramatic work, and friends", which, for Caitlin meant "flattery, idleness, and infidelity". In one of his last radio pieces *A Visit to*

America, Dylan made humorous fun of his experiences on the lecture circuit. He was by then a veteran of three extensive tours during which he gave just over a hundred lectures and readings across the States (and he had only failed to make it to one). Here is one bravura section from an amazing broadcast:

A rare snap of Dylan and Caitlin travelling across America

There they go, every spring, from New York to Los Angeles: exhibitionists, polemicists, histrionic publicists, theological rhetoricians, historical hoddy-doddies, balletomanes, ulterior decorators, max-factored actors, windbags, and bigwigs and humbugs, men in love with stamps, men in love with steaks, men after millionaires' widows, men with elephantiasis of the reputation (huge trunks and teeny minds).

The rant goes on and on, but it ends with a telling note of self-deprecation:

potboiling philosophers, professional Irishmen (very lepri-corny) and, I am afraid, fat poets with slim volumes.

With a cruel irony the BBC scheduled this broadcast to go out on the day of Dylan's funeral and it had to be postponed until March 1954. James A Davies sums it up:

The USA was the setting for the most destructive part of his almost-eager pilgrimage to that small hotel room in New York and Alcohol's lethal coma.

A recently discovered and previously unpublished photo of Dylan and Caitlin in a New York bar, with Rose and Dave Slivka – the sculptor who would make Dylan's death mask

The White Horse Tavern

Corner of Hudson and 11th Street, New York City

PERCHED on the western edge of Greenwich Village, the White Horse Tavern is one of the few wood-framed buildings remaining in Manhattan. The tavern has inhabited the same site since the late 19th century when it replaced an even older Oyster House, and it is one of the oldest bars in New York City. For decades, its proximity to the warehouses and docks of the Hudson made it a longshoreman's hangout, with no literary ambiance whatsoever. However in the late forties, Greenwich Village began to attract writers and artists, poets and bohemians, who could find cheap accommodation in the huge disused lofts and tenements of the neighbourhood. The White Horse began to take on a new clientele and a new atmosphere. The presence of the local workforce kept the place grounded. However tensions with the blue collar regulars meant that the change was not without incident.

In *New York in the 50s*, author Dan Wakefield writes:

> The hostility toward all nonconformists was heightened during the McCarthy fervour of the Fifties, when mostly Irish kids from the surrounding area made raids on the Horse, swinging fists and chairs, calling the regulars "commies and faggots".

Wakefield himself was a political activist who kept alive this political dimension. He would go to the White Horse after Dorothy Day's militant pacifist lectures at the Catholic Worker Hospitality House. There he would knock back pints and join in songs of the Irish rebellions and the Spanish Civil War with the Irish folk group the Clancy Brothers or with Mary Travers, the statuesque blonde who became one-third of the popular 1960s folk trio Peter, Paul and Mary. Wakefield remembers the White Horse in the 50s as a bar where:

> you could always find a friend, join a conversation, relax and feel you were part of a community.

The fact that the bar was more like a British pub than many other American bars led to it becoming a popular haunt with visiting British travellers. Before Dylan Thomas arrived, it was a favourite with the actor Charles Laughton and his patronage began creating the legend. For Laughton it was a wonderful, quiet pub with good beer; fabulous roast beef sandwiches for 35 cents; a cribbage board on the bar so you could play the bartender for drinks; and beer served in curious heavy-bottomed mugs. Laughton loved the place, and

Thomas
2012   WHITE HORSE TAVERN
        NEW YORK

one night just before he was going to catch a liner to England, he decided it needed some publicity. He bought 300 of the White Horse mugs and passed them out the next day on board ship. That did it. The people to whom he gave the mugs were intrigued, they cherished the mugs and told their friends about the bar; the legend of the White Horse had started.

The unique White Horse Tavern beer pot

This was about three years before Dylan Thomas added to the bar's growing charisma. He was introduced to the bar on his first trip to America by his old London friend Ruthven Todd, who had relocated to New York and was an established writer and artist well known in the village. The Horse was Todd's bar of choice and he was eager to share its pleasures with his old friend. The pub's waterside location appealed to Dylan; throughout his life so many of his homes and haunts were close to water, but then the boy Dylan in Welsh myth is described as 'son of wave.' John Malcolm Brinnin observed that the White Horse:

> was as homely and dingy as many a London pub and perhaps just as old.

The pub's ambience and clientele was much like the pubs he first loved in Swansea's dockside and the Horse began to provide for him some kind of comforting home from home when the rigours and terrors of New York threatened to overwhelm him as they often did. He described them to his parents:

> this titanic dream world, soaring Babylon... this mad city... the nightmare city.

The tavern attracted other writers; novelists Norman Mailer and James Baldwin drank there, and Anais Nin, who was New York's equivalent of London's Nina Hamnett, was one of the few women writers who hung out at the Horse. Seymour Krim, the early *Village Voice* writer, whose collected pieces *Views of a Near-Sighted Cannoneer* helped spawn the New Journalism of the late 60s, hung out in the Horse. In fact the idea for the *Voice* seems to have been incubated there, and its offices were eventually established on nearby Sheridan Square. While Dylan and his friends were patronising the Village, down on the east side Bowery area, holed up in seamy steamy apartments, were the young guns of the next generation – The Beats. But they sometimes ventured into Greenwich Village: Allan Ginsberg, who met Dylan in the nearby San Remo bar, and Gregory Corso, who visited Dylan when he lay in his fatal coma in nearby Saint Vincent's Hospital.

When Jack Kerouac was famously writing *On The Road* on a continuous roll of teletype paper, he used to drink so heavily at the White Horse that he was often thrown out and banned. In his later book *Desolation Angels,* Kerouac writes of his shock when he discovered

"Go Home Kerouac" scrawled on a wall in the men's room.

Kenneth Rexroth, the poet and central figure in the San Francisco Renaissance, which paved the way for the Beat movement, wrote a powerful lament for the death of Dylan Thomas and a frontal attack on bourgeois hypocrisy entitled *Thou Shalt Not Kill*. This poem, which Rexroth would perform to a free jazz accompaniment, is seen as a major influence on Ginsberg's seminal Beat poem *Howl*. Rexroth cites Dylan Thomas and the great jazz saxophonist Charlie Parker as being:

> the Godfathers of the Beat Generation.

Other famous patrons included poet Delmore Schwartz, the writer Richard Farina who died young but wrote the beat classic *Been Down so Long it Looks Like Up to Me* (and a short story that mentions Dylan Thomas). Mr *Fear and Loathing* himself, Hunter S Thompson, was known to enjoy the bar. And we cannot forget one Robert Zimmerman, a young folk singer who blew into New York City at the start of the burgeoning folk music craze, just a few years after Dylan Thomas had died there. He would change his name to Bob Dylan in homage to a certain Welsh poet; he also drank in the White Horse Tavern.

The bar has another Swansea connection. The 60s chanteuse from the Swansea Valley, Mary Hopkin, one-time girlfriend of Paul McCartney, had her one

Dylan enjoying a jar with a couple of locals – the Horse served its beer in idiosyncratic heavy ceramic mugs

huge hit record on the Beatles' new Apple record label with the song *Those Were the Days*. It was a cover of a song by Gene Raskin, who had adapted it from a Russian folk song of the 1920s. The opening line, "Once upon a time there was a Tavern", refers to the White Horse.

Sadly the great bar is now remembered not just as Dylan's favourite New York bar but the bar where he began the drinking binge that led to his untimely death. It has become a place of pilgrimage for many people from around the world who read, admire, and are inspired by Dylan Thomas's poetry.

Dylan as Bob

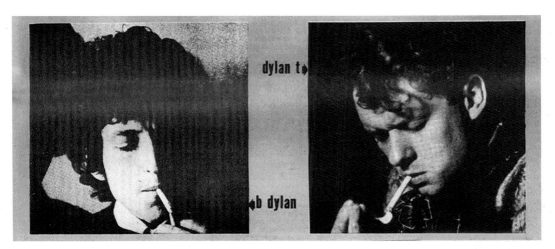

Bob Dylan and Dylan Thomas inexplicably but permanently linked by a Welsh name

The tragic, poignant last photograph of Dylan Thomas in the White Horse Tavern – the beer pots are left on the counter and it is whiskey shots for Dylan now. In a few days he would be dead

The White Horse today

The White Horse Tavern now attracts students and tourists rather than longshoremen and writers. Visitors can still look about the bar area and can see at least a dozen white horses; the most prominent stares down at customers from the wall behind the mirrored bar and was put there to advertise the still-served White Horse Whiskey. And white horse heads perch in a circle on the top of chandeliers and tiny white ivory horses are bucking and cantering along most of the ledges and shelves.

Occasionally writers like Frank McCourt, author of the best-selling *Angela's Ashes*, will call in for a drink and before his tragic early death, John Belushi often sat at the White Horse bar. The night Belushi died in 1982 his *Saturday Night Live* partner, Dan Akroyd, walked into the tavern at closing time, shut the doors and bought the entire bar a round of drinks. Belushi himself was deeply fascinated by Dylan Thomas and bought the rights to make a film of his life. It actually began production with Gary Oldman as Dylan and Uma Thurman as Caitlin. Filming had begun in Laugharne, using the Boathouse as a location, when the leading man was taken seriously ill; the project stalled and the whole film was abandoned. The few remaining rough-cuts suggest it is perhaps a lost masterpiece.

The bar's other draw, besides its rich literary history, is its architecture and design. The tin ceiling is hand-engraved and still bears the painted-over scars of the ripped out and replaced gaslight equipment. The serving bar itself is the original, carved out of a single piece of mahogany. Today it offers good American bar meals which come in Desperate Dan-sized portions and a wide selection of ales and Hefeweizens (wheat beers). Add to this a well stocked classic jukebox offering an eclectic selection ranging from Morrissey to Santana, Radiohead to Counting Crows, it is a bar that rewards the literary pilgrim and general tourist alike.

The Copley Plaza

Boston

THE FAIRMONT COPLEY PLAZA had been a symbol of Boston's rich history and elegance since its gala opening in 1912. It was not the sort of place where Dylan often found himself. He was in Boston on his third trip in 1953 and had given two readings at the prestigious Fogg Museum in Harvard – one had been a mixed programme of poetry and Shakespeare, and the other, a trial solo performance of the almost completed *Under Milk Wood*. At the same time, and by complete coincidence, Igor Stravinsky was in Boston to conduct Boston University students in two performances of his neoclassical opera *The Rake's Progress*. The dean of the university asked Stravinsky if he would consider a commission from them to compose a new opera. He was indeed interested. The libretto for *The Rake's Progress* had been written by Aldous Huxley and he had suggested to the composer that Dylan Thomas might make a future collaborator. Given the opportunity by Boston University, Stravinsky proposed Dylan as his librettist.

Boston University's proposal was not the first to attempt to set up a collaboration between the composer and the poet. In 1952 the British film producer Michael Powell had approached Stravinsky to write the music for a movie based on a scene from *The Odyssey* and Dylan would write the script. But this had not materialised; Stravinsky would later write:

> Alas, there was no money. Where were the angels, even the Broadway kind, and why are the world's commissions, grants, funds, foundations never available to the Dylan Thomases?

In 1953 Dylan was in dire need of an angel. His life was in turmoil; his drinking was increasing with his worries; his health was not good and he couldn't hold on to any of the money he made. He could not find the money for his children's education and officials from the Inland Revenue were hounding him. On May 21st, 1953, it looked like those up above had noticed his plight when this telegram arrived:

LE CÉLÈBRE COMPOSITEUR
IGOR STRAWINSKI
(exclusivité Columbia)

Would you agree in principle to compose an opera libretto for Igor Stravinsky?

Boston University could offer him $1500 up front and $1500 on completion of the libretto. Thus Dylan found himself in the plush confines of the Copley Plaza where the great composer was staying. Dylan found Stravinsky in bed, recovering from two strenuous concert performances. They were ill-matched partners: Stravinsky, at seventy-two, was fastidious and precise, a dapper dresser, a disciplined worker. Dylan was his usual somewhat unfocussed self and looking, as always, "like an unmade bed". But the two men clicked. In his book *Conversations* (1959), Stravinsky writes:

> As soon as I saw him I knew that the only thing to do was to love him... He was nervous, however, chain-smoking the whole time... His nose was a red bulb, and his eyes were glazed. He drank a glass of whiskey with me, which made him more at ease, though he kept worrying about his wife saying he had to hurry home to Wales "or it would be too late".

"His" opera was to be about the rediscovery of our planet after "an atomic misadventure".

In *Dylan Thomas in America,* Brinnin describes how enthused and excited Dylan was by the prospect of working with such a great avant-garde musician:

> Dylan was immensely pleased and, I could see, not a little flattered to have been considered for the assignment... I had seldom observed him in so buoyant a state of creative agitation.

PLEY PLAZA HOTEL . BOSTON .

Even more importantly, Dylan could tell Caitlin of the project and boast:

> That's not just optimistic: it can, & will be. In advance, I'll be given 500 pounds & our passage first class, & then another £500 – & then royalties until we die.

A plan was hatched that Dylan would to return to Wales and then make another short tour of the East Coast in the autumn, mainly to reprise *Under Milk Wood* in New York. Then Caitlin would join him and they would both travel to Los Angeles, where Stravinsky was building a lodge for them in his garden and he and Dylan could begin work on their opera. On June 22nd, Stravinsky wrote to Thomas agreeing that he should come in September or October. A week later Stravinsky heard that the university was having trouble raising the funds and his reply sought to reassure them:

> We will not deliver a work involving an outrageously expensive staging (not another "Aida" for example). We can be committed to deliver a work whose production will require only a limited chamber ensemble, a limited number of characters and small chorus members.

On August 26th Stravinsky suggested that Thomas come regardless of whether or not Boston University could come up with the money. A month later he wrote to say that he'd ask his friends Aldous Huxley and Christopher Isherwood to help set up lectures for Thomas, and he concluded:

> I am as eager as you are to actually see "our" (yes) work started. Bon voyage. A bientot.

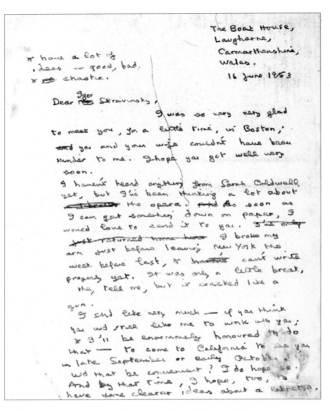

Dylan's excitement is evident in this draft letter: "I have a lot of ideas – good, bad and chaotic".

Thomas flew to New York on October 19th. On November 9th he was dead. What might have been? The following year saw the première of Stravinsky's newest work *In Memoriam: Dylan Thomas*. This setting of *Do Not Go Gentle Into That Good Night* was the only bitter fruit of a collaboration that never happened.

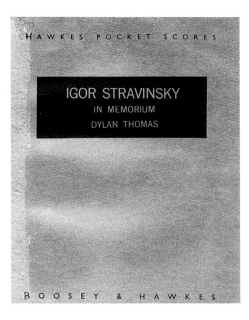

HAWKES POCKET SCORES

IGOR STRAVINSKY
IN MEMORIUM
DYLAN THOMAS

BOOSEY & HAWKES

The Copley is still one of Boston's finest hotels and it was where Richard Burton and Elizabeth Taylor chose to spend their honeymoon after their wedding in 1964, when they were at the height of their global celebrity. Some accounts of the event describe scenes of manic chaos as rabid crowds clawed at the newlyweds; Burton's coat was ripped and Taylor's ear was bloodied when someone tried to steal one of her earrings. Sadly, it was recently at the epicentre of the terrorist bomb attack on the finishing line of the Boston Marathon. However it has stoically remained open and welcoming.

On a lighter note, Stravinsky did provoke Dylan to enjoy some music in Boston, albeit of a much different kind. Brinnin describes how, after Dylan's first meeting with Stravinsky in the Copley, he and Dylan enjoyed a good dinner washed down by a fine bottle of *Vin Rosé* that Stravinsky had given to Dylan as a token to seal their collaboration. Dylan, in a very upbeat mood then asked Brinnin to drive him to a Boston nightclub where the great early pop idol Johnnie Ray was performing. Dylan wanted to be able to boast of this to Caitlin, who was a big Johnnie Ray fan.

The Players Restaurant

8225 Sunset Boulevard, Hollywood, Los Angeles

DYLAN THOMAS only made one visit to Los Angeles in April of 1950, on his first tour. He gave a reading at UCLA, and he did manage to make it to Hollywood and meet a few celebrities. As always there are wildly differing accounts of just what Dylan got up on his short stay in the city... and the adventure started in the Players Restaurant.

The Players was developed by the great film director Preston Sturges, who gave us a group of laugh-out-loud, politically-tinged, crazy comedies: *Sullivan's Travels*, *The Palm Beach Story* and *The Lady Eve*, among many others. The Players operated at 8225 Sunset Boulevard. It formed a triangle with two other legendary establishments: Chateau Marmont was next door, and across the road was the Garden of Allah complex.

From 1940 to 1953, The Players multilevel supper club, frequented by Humphrey Bogart, Orson Welles, Dorothy Parker and Howard Hughes, was a nexus of the Hollywood aristocracy, who all enjoyed its louche atmosphere and cocktails, said to be the most potent in town.

Dylan Thomas was unaware of any of this when he found himself stranded at the Biltmore Hotel in Los Angeles with no means of finding his way to the UCLA campus to give his reading to the English department, who had failed to provide any transport for him. Somewhere in his luggage he found a scrap of paper with a contact number for Christopher Isherwood, the writer and friend of Auden and Huxley. Isherwood took pity on Dylan and picked him up, drove him to the campus, and stayed to give him moral support throughout the evening. The two then made their way back to the Players where two other old London mates were waiting for him, the screenwriter Ivan Moffat, who Dylan drank with back in the Gargoyle days, and Frank Taylor, a publisher and producer. They were determined to show their old pal a Hollywood good time and asked Dylan what he most wanted to do.

Dylan's response to this unexpected magic lamp was to demand just two, rather than the customary three wishes. Dylan loved films, from childhood Saturday morning kids' film shows to his later regular visits to small art house cinemas to watch Gothic horrors and Marx brothers comedies. His great hero was always Charlie Chaplin; he seemed to identify with Chaplin's onscreen character and his friends sometimes likened Dylan to him. At his last public appearance in New York, at the Cinema 16 symposium on "Film and Poetry", Dylan proclaimed that Charles Chaplin made the most "poetic films".

So wish number one was to meet Charlie Chaplin. Wish number two was a tad more predictable; he wanted to meet "the most beautiful blonde in Hollywood". That may have been extreme wishful thinking on his part, but his friends had the wherewithal to satisfy both his demands in one fell swoop. Both Moffat and Isherwood had worked with the buxom blonde Shelley Winters, so when she arrived at the restaurant they called her over to join them – and Winters was a friend of Chaplin's.

Like so many episodes in Dylan's life there are many accounts of the next twenty-four hours and no two of them match up. One of the greatest books I ever handled in my bookselling days was the actual book that Dylan inscribed and presented to Chaplin on the night they met. This is my bookseller's description of the volume:

DYLAN THOMAS TO CHARLIE CHAPLIN: A REMARKABLE PRESENTATION COPY

Thomas, Dylan; Selected Writings. 1946. New Directions. First edition, first issue. A very good copy in dust jacket with a bold full page inscription on the f.e.p. Written in green ink, in what can only be described as a drunken scrawl by Dylan, to his great hero Charlie Chaplin;

L A
& love
homage
to & for
Charles Chaplin
From
Dylan Thomas
1950

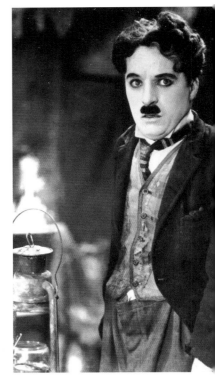

I treasured and kept the book for years, but when I decided to sell it I also decided to try and get absolute top dollar for it. To achieve this I had to provide solid provenance and a good back story. The book had provenance enough. It had been bought by a bookseller colleague of mine from one of Chaplin's children, who lived near her business, and I had bought it directly from her. But any prospective collector would want more detail.

When I began to look into this I found that most all the participants in the evening's events had written up and published their own accounts and, would you believe? no two matched in any way – other than to confirm that Dylan Thomas had indeed met Shelley Winters and had gone on to meet Chaplin. Isherwood, Moffat, Winters and Charlie himself, had all written accounts in their respective autobiographies. Subsequently John Malcolm Brinnin, Fitzgibbon,

Ferris and Lycett, together with all of Dylan's other biographers, each of them covered the story, and they all describe a different sequence of events. Dylan Thomas writes about his meeting with Chaplin in two letters to Caitlin:

April 18, 1950

Went to Hollywood, dined with Charlie Chaplin, saw Ivan Moffat, stayed with Christopher Isherwood, was ravingly miserable for you my true, my dear, my one, my precious love. I shall write to Llewelyn too tomorrow.

May 7, 1950

I am glad Charlie Chaplin wired to you. He said he wanted to send his greetings. He's a very fine man. I was only 2 days in Hollywood, staying with Christopher Isherwood who took me along to Chaplin's to dinner. Chaplin danced & clowned all the time. I met also Ivan Moffat. Ivan says I could get a script to write almost any time. Once we are in San Francisco, we will see: it is not far away.

The juiciest account of the event is that given by Shelley Winters, in her 1990 biography, *Best of Times Worst of Times:*

One night, when I showed up exhausted from filming *Frenchie*, complete with platinum hair and padded bra, Christopher Isherwood and Ivan Moffat were seated with an ugly, funny-handsome young Welshman. He had very black, curly, almost kinky hair, rather a stocky build (just a little taller than I), and very rumpled clothes. He was altogether charming, and I gathered it was his first night in Hollywood. His name was something Thomas – I didn't catch the first part but since we were retaking a scene the next day, and I didn't have to learn any new lines, I could enjoy the conversation with this cute Welshman.

When I asked Mr Thomas what he did, Ivan told me, "He draws accurate and biting images of people and events." So I assumed he was a cartoonist, and they all let me assume this for a long time. The young man, of course, was Dylan Thomas, but he didn't look like any writer I had ever met in Hollywood. In those days writers wore suits and ties. My friends told me he was working for some London newspaper. In the course of dinner, I asked Mr Thomas why he had come to Hollywood. He looked deep into my blue eyes and whispered sexily, "To touch the titties of a beautiful blonde starlet and to meet Charlie Chaplin."

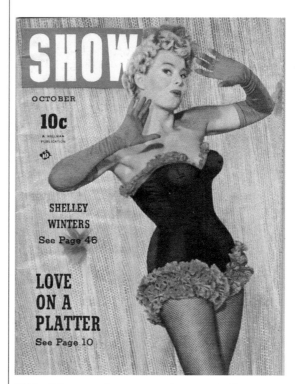

Shirley Winters makes an attractive cover for Show *magazine*

I gazed at the two literary figures beside us. They said nothing. "Okay," I said, "I can grant both your wishes." When we had finished the dessert and brandy, I announced, "You may touch each of my breasts with one finger, and the day after tomorrow will be Sunday, and Charlie Chaplin has open house, as Christopher and Ivan well know. I will take you up there."

Ivan bought us a bottle of champagne and poured it. Then, with great ceremony, Mr Thomas sterilized his index finger in the champagne and delicately brushed each breast with the finger, leaving a streak in my pancake body makeup. A look of supreme ecstasy came over this Welsh elf's face. "Oh, God, Nirvana," he uttered. "I do not believe it's necessary for me to meet Charlie Chaplin now." Christopher and Ivan were laughing uproariously. I knew I was being joshed, and I informed my dinner companions that the brakes on my car were not too good, and since Charlie was on top of Summit Ridge Drive, we could pass on that trip. "No, no," said Ivan. "I've loaned Dylan my green Hornet while he's in California, and if you keep him on the right side of the road, he can drive you up to the Chaplin house Sunday night. He really is longing to meet Charlie, and I'm sure Charlie is anxious to meet him."

Why Chaplin would want to meet this obscure Welsh cartoonist was as a mystery to me. Also he just sat there when the check came, so it was obvious he had very little money. So I invited him to an early Sunday dinner the next night with me and my then-roommate, Marilyn Monroe. Then we would all drive up to Charlie's house after dinner. By the time I left the Players that night, I realized that Mr Thomas had a serious drinking problem, and, if Ivan or Christopher couldn't drive us up to Charlie Chapin's house, I decided I would drive the green Hornet myself...

Christopher Isherwood and Ivan Moffat were pretending they didn't know Dylan and me, but suddenly everyone was looking at Dylan and wanted to talk to him. Since he was very drunk, I couldn't think why. He, on the other hand, obviously didn't want to talk to anybody but Charlie Chaplin. Charlie was sitting at the piano, playing a strange, beautiful tune. I quickly went over to Ivan and Christopher and asked them why they had asked me to take care of their difficult, drunken cartoonist friend. With a very straight face, as was his wont, Ivan asked me if I didn't like Mr Thomas? "When he's relatively sober, he's adorable," I replied. "But he has a terrible drinking problem, doesn't he? Perhaps I should make an appointment for him with a good Beverly Hills psychiatrist."

Dylan Thomas abruptly got up. And I slid to the floor. He suddenly seemed cold sober and took Charlie junior's hands and danced around the room with him, humming the tune in his melodious voice. Charlie junior kept right on la-la-la-ing off-key and sort of sarcastically Charlie senior crashed his hands on the keyboard, got up, and knocked Charlie junior's hands away from Dylan. Unable to distinguish who was doing what, Charlie senior hissed at Dylan, "Even great poetry cannot excuse such rude, drunken behavior."

Dylan turned on his heel and, in a very dignified manner, walked out into the solarium. Charlie junior sat on a hassock and began to weep bitterly. "Sydney is playing the lead in the film," he screamed. "I won't be an extra. I won't, I won't." As the guests left hurriedly, we heard a sound like running water. Dylan was peeing on a large plant on Charlie's porch. In this decade I seem to have known a lot of gentlemen who peed as an act of revenge.

This account is the only one to throw Marilyn Monroe into the mix, and have Dylan driving, – Dylan driving? But then the image of Dylan Thomas careering down Hollywood freeways in a borrowed green Hornet, obviously a convertible, with the blonde tresses of Monroe and Winters entwining in the wind, is both too much to take – or ignore!

By contrast here is Chaplin's short restrained version from his *My Autobiography* (1964):

> One day, our friend Frank Taylor telephoned to say that Dylan Thomas, the Welsh poet, would like to meet us. We said we would be delighted. "Well," said Frank hesitantly, "I'll bring him round if he's sober". Later that evening when the bell rang I opened the door and Dylan Thomas fell in; if this was being sober, what would he be like when he was drunk? A day or so later he came to dinner and made better sense. He read to us one of his poems, rendered in a deep resonant voice. I do not remember the imagery, but the word "cellophane" flashed like reflected sunshine from his magical verse.

As for the sale of my copy of the book Dylan presented to Chaplin, I gathered up and collated all the variant accounts, some dozen versions by a dozen writers. It amounted to a sizable dossier, which I printed off and sent, with the book, to the bold Irishman who whispered down the phone in a soft Dublin lilt:

> What would be your very best price for a poor Irish farmer who loves great books?

He got the book, which is the tangible proof of an extraordinary meeting, but will we ever know what really transpired that night? As is so often the case with Dylan Thomas – somewhere between these many accounts lies some kind of truth.

The Players Restaurant today

The original Preston Sturges restaurant closed in 1953, and sadly, much of the glamour that was the Players exists only in the memories of a few of the older Hollywood doyens and in film fan magazines and vintage photographs of the era. The original site has since played host to numerous clubs and eateries and it has recently been re-opened by Harry Morton – son of Hard Rock Café founder Peter Morton – as the second LA outpost of his Mexican restaurant chain Pink Taco.

Bibliography of works consulted

WORKS BY DYLAN THOMAS

18 Poems. Sunday Referee, 1934.
Twenty-Five Poems. London: Dent, 1936.
The Map of Love. London: Dent, 1939.
Portrait of the Artist as a Young Dog. London: Dent, 1940.
New Poems. Norfolk, CT: New Directions, 1943.
Deaths and Entrances. London: Dent, 1946.
Collected Poems, 1934-1952. London: Dent, 1952.
Quite Early One Morning. London: Dent, 1954.
Under Milk Wood. Preface by Daniel Jones. 1954. London: Dent/Everyman, 1992.
A Prospect of the Sea. Ed. Daniel Jones. London: Dent, 1955.
Adventures in the Skin Trade. Aldine paperback ed. 1955. London: Dent, 1965.
Letters to Vernon Watkins. Ed. Vernon Watkins. London: Dent and Faber & Faber, 1957.
The Beach of Falesá. 1964. New York: Stein and Day, 1983.
Twenty Years A-Growing. London: Dent, 1964.
Rebecca's Daughters. 1965. London.
The Doctor and the Devils, and Other Scripts. New York: New Directions, 1966.
Poet in the Making: The Notebooks of Dylan Thomas. Ed. Ralph Maud. London: Dent, 1968.
Early Prose Writings. Ed. Walford Davies. London: Dent, 1971.
The Poems. Ed. Daniel Jones. Revised ed, 1974. London: Dent, 1982.
The Death of the King's Canary (with John Davenport). 1976.
Collected Stories. Ed. Walford Davies. 1983. London: Dent/Everyman, 1995.
The Collected Letters. Ed. Paul Ferris. London: Dent, 1985 (new edition 2000).
Collected Poems, 1934-1953. Ed. Walford Davies and Ralph Maud. London: Dent, 1988.
The Notebook Poems, 1930-34. Ed. Ralph Maud. London: Dent, 1989.
The Broadcasts. Ed. Ralph Maud. London: Dent, 1991.
Letter to Loren. Ed. Jeff Towns. Swansea: Salubrious Press, 1993.
The Filmscripts. Ed. John Ackerman. London: Dent, 1995.
Under Milk Wood. Ed. Walford Davies, Ralph Maud. Definitive edition, London: Dent, 1995.

WORKS ON DYLAN THOMAS

Ackerman, John. *Dylan Thomas: His Life and Work*. 1964.
Ackerman, John. *Welsh Dylan*. 1979.
Ackerman, John. *A Dylan Thomas Companion*. Basingstoke: Macmillan, 1991.

Brinnin, John Malcolm. *Dylan Thomas in America.* London: Dent, 1956.

Brinnin, John Malcolm. (Ed.) *A Casebook on Dylan Thomas.* New York: Crowell, 1960.

Cleverdon, Douglas. *The Growth of "Milk Wood".* London: Dent, 1969.

Davies, Aneirin Talfan. *Dylan: Druid of the Broken Body.* London: Dent, 1964.

Davies, James A. "Crying in My Wordy Wilderness". Anglo-Welsh Review 83 (1986): 96-105.

Davies, James A. *Dylan Thomas's Places: A Biographical and Literary Guide.* Swansea: Christopher Davies, 1987.

Davies, James A. *A Reference Companion to Dylan Thomas.* Greenwood Press, 1998.

Davies, Walford. *Dylan Thomas.* Revised ed, Cardiff: University of Wales Press, 1990.

Davies, Walford. (Ed.). *Dylan Thomas: New Critical Essays.* London: Dent, 1972.

Davies, Walford. *Dylan Thomas.* Milton Keynes: Open University Press, 1986.

Ferris, Paul. *Dylan Thomas: The Biography.* Talybont: Y Lolfa, 2006 (reprint).

Ferris, Paul. *Caitlin: The Life of Caitlin Thomas.* London: Hutchinson, 1993.

Fuller, Jean Overton. *The Magical Dilemma of Victor Neuberg.* Allen, 1965.

FitzGibbon, Constantine. *The Life of Dylan Thomas.* London: Dent, 1965.

Gittins, Rob. The Last Days of Dylan Thomas. Macdonald, 1986.

Johnson, Pamela Hansford. *Important to Me: Personalia.* London: Macmillan, 1974.

Jones, Daniel. *My Friend Dylan Thomas.* London: Dent, 1977.

Jones, Glyn. *The Dragon Has Two Tongues.* London: Dent, 1968.

Lewis, Min. *Laugharne and Dylan Thomas.* Dobson, 1967.

McKenna, Rollie. *Portrait of Dylan.* Dent 1982.

Maud, Ralph. (Ed.) *Wales in His Arms: Dylan Thomas's Choice of Welsh Poetry.* Cardiff: University of Wales Press, 1994.

Read, Bill. *The Days of Dylan Thomas.* London: Weidenfeld & Nicolson, 1964.

Sinclair Andrew. *Dylan Thomas: Poet of His People.* Michael Joseph 1975. New edition.

Dylan the Bard. Constable 2000.

Seymour, Tryntje. *Dylan Thomas' New York.* Stemmer. 1977.

Stanford, Derek. *Dylan Thomas.* 1954. Revised and extended ed, New York: Citadel Press, 1964.

Tedlock, E. W. (Ed.). *Dylan Thomas: The Legend and the Poet.* London: William Heinemann, 1960.

Thomas, Caitlin. *Leftover Life to Kill.* London: Putnam, 1957.

Thomas, Caitlin. *Not Quite Posthumous Letter to My Daughter.* London: Putnam, 1963.

Thomas, Caitlin with Tremlett, George. *Caitlin: A Warring Absence.* London: Seeker, 1986.

Thomas, Caitlin. *Double Drink Story.* Virago Press 1998.

Todd, Rudven. *Fitzrovia and the Road to York Minster.* Parkin Finer Art, 1973.

Towns, Jeff. *Word and Image*. Dylan Thomas Centre. Swansea: 1995.

Tremlett, George. *Dylan Thomas: In the Mercy of His Means*. London: Constable, 1991.

Trick, Bert. "The Young Dylan Thomas". Texas *Quarterly 9* (Summer 1966): 36-49.

Watkins, Gwen. *Portrait of a Friend*. Talybont: Y Lolfa, 1983.

BACKGROUND BOOKS

Clancy, Liam. *Memoirs of an Irish Troubadour*. Virgin 2002.

Davies, Brian E. *Mumbles and Gower Pubs*. Tempus 2006.

Davies, James A. *Dylan Thomas's Swansea, Gower and Laugharne*. UWP 2000.

Davin, Dan. *Closing Times*. OUP, 1975.

Farson, Daniel. *Soho in the Fifties*. Michael Joseph, 1987.

Fitzgibbon, Theodora. *With Love: An Autobiography*. Century London, 1982.

Fryer, Jonathan. *Soho in the Fifties* and Sixties. NPG, 1998.

Fuller, Jean Overton. *The Magical Dilemma of Victor Neuberg*. W.H. Allen, 1965.

Hawkins, Desmond. *When I was*. Macmillan, 1989.

Heppenstall, Rayner. *Four Absentees*. Barrie and Rockliff, 1969.

Holroyd, Michael. *Augustus John*. Heinemann, 1974.

Holt, Heather. *Dylan Thomas the Actor*. Published by the author. Swansea: 2003.

Hudson, Roger. *Bloomsbury, Fitzrovia & Soho*. Haggerson Press, 1996.

Isherwood, Christopher. *Diaries. Volume One, 1939-1960*.

Jenkins, Nigel. *Real Swansea*. Seren, 2008.

Lindsay, Jack. *Meetings with Poets*. Muller, 1968.

Maclaren-Ross, Julian. *Memoirs of the Forties*. Alan Ross, 1965.

Pentelow & Rowe. *Characters of Fitzrovia*. Chatto and Windus 2001.

Sinclair, Upton. *The Cup of Fury*. Chanel Press, 1956.

Stanford Derek. *Inside the Forties*. Sidgwick & Jackson, 1977.

Summers, John. *DYLAN: a novel*. NEL, 1970.

Thomas Aeronwy. *My Father's Places*. Constable, 2009.

Thomas, D N. *A Farm, Two Mansions and a Bungalow*. Seren, 2000.

Edits. *Dylan Remembered*. The Colin Edwards Interviews. 2003/4. *Fatal Neglect*. Seren.

Vaughan Thomas, Wynford. *Madly in All Directions*. Longmans, 1967.

Watkins, Dorothy. *Vernon Phillips Watkins: The Early Years*.

Willetts, Paul. *Fear and Loathing in Fitzrovia*. Dewi Lewis, 2003.

Also published by Y Lolfa:

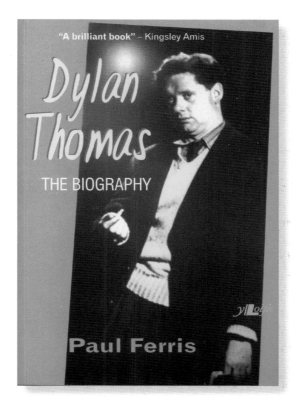

Paul Ferris' authoritative and widely acclaimed biography of Dylan Thomas.
0 86243 903 5
£12.95

...and Gwen Watkins' honest memoir:

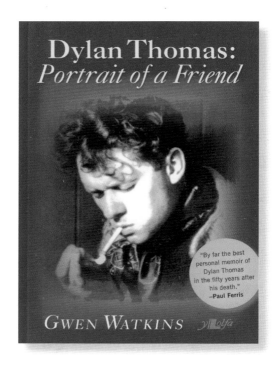

"She looks at Dylan and her husband, Vernon Watkins, with an angry candour that makes this by far the best personal memoir of Dylan Thomas in the fifty years after his death." – Paul Ferris

0 86243 780 6

£9.95

*For a full list of publications, simply surf into our website, **www.ylolfa.com.***